MODUS VIVENDI
The road to happiness, freedom and peace

Other Books by the Author

POETRY

Odes to a Goddess
Poems and Gems of Love
Petals of Love
Flames of Love
Songs of Love
Echoes

NOVELS

Sandora
In the Silence of Love

SHORT STORIES

Intriguing Short Stories of Love and Lust
A Matter of Immorality: A collection of Short Stories

HUMANISM

Beliefs and Thoughts

MODUS VIVENDI

The road to happiness, freedom and peace

Ramkarrun Jokhoo

ATHENA PRESS
LONDON

Dedicated to the seekers of peace, happiness and freedom.

Introduction, by Mark Sykes

*M*odus Vivendi is an eloquent yet accessible continuation of the themes of Divine Humanism established in *Beliefs and Thoughts*.

With a clarity that is at once disarming and engaging, Jokhoo offers ethical, moral and political guidance to a spiritually bankrupt world. But what makes *Modus Vivendi* uniquely useful is not theoretical or abstract; it is its practicality, its very real solutions to managing the most difficult of human relationships: individual with State; individual with society; individual with family; individual with God.

With gentle persuasion and practical example, Jokhoo quickly captures his readers and carries them along on a current of common sense that is on occasion so straightforward its very simplicity makes it oblique until the author reveals the truth, as though from behind a hazy gauze:

> …we know we must be polite, yet we are rude; we know we must love one another, yet we hate one another or pretend to love one another; we know we must not be greedy, yet we want more than our needs…

And once the truth has been revealed, without condescension or judgement Jokhoo shows us the way.

Through careful anthropological study, Jokhoo takes us back to a time when men were noble and the world a happy, peaceful place to be and examines what we need to change – as individuals; as husbands/wives; as sons/daughters; as humans in the most noble sense – need to do to recapture this golden age.

Mark Sykes

Consultant Editor-in-Chief, Athena Press

Contents

Human Relationships

I am told there are 840,000 living species in the universe, and a human being is, overall, rated the most advanced and the most superior of them. Since I am one of the top rated species, I consider myself fortunate and blessed. Being superior to any other species, I must live up to my status in this hierarchy through my actions. If they do not match my status, I am not a human being: I am either a saint, a god or an animal of a lower ranking. But I am none of these, so what must my actions be?

In the course of his or her life, a human being performs many actions. One of them, and probably the most important of them, is to form a relationship with other human beings, with animals and with objects. A relationship can be either good or bad. A bad one is transient, lasting only until it is recognised as bad. For example, a relationship with a so-called friend whose intention is to befriend you first, and then to make off with something that belongs to you – which is money in most cases – cannot be permanent.

A bad relationship is also destructive. In the above example, it destroys the love and the trust that one has for the other; it destroys the plan devised for the stolen money; and it destroys the happiness of the cheated friend. It causes hatred, selfishness and anger. It breeds enmity, vengeance and misanthropy. It harbours those undesirable instincts that men, through ages, have unfortunately allowed to grow in them, and which now they can neither control nor eradicate. It is this destructive force that prompts me to probe the good side of a relationship and find a solution for its bad side.

Forming a relationship is inevitable. A person's first relationship is with his mother and it starts even before he is born. In her womb she provides him with comfort, protection and nourishment – a duty she carries out with extraordinary maternal love and care. She does not neglect him in the least bit after he is born.

On the contrary, she performs this duty with more enthusiasm and resolve. She gives him a lot more because she knows more is needed for his upbringing.

She teaches him how to establish a good relationship with other members of the family, what is good for him and how to behave in different situations and circumstances. She inculcates these qualities in him from his very birth. She feeds him at calculated, regular intervals; likewise she lulls him to sleep; and she changes him when he requires changing. She spends a lot of her time with him and thus a mother–child bond is permanently established. Projection of this bond is important for him, as it is the basis of his relationship with his elders and other members of the family, his friends, his teachers and the members of his community.

The mother teaches her child to control destructive qualities such as anger, impatience, hatred, rudeness and insolence. With love and kindness, she achieves her aim and earns his respect and gratitude. It must not be forgotten that a mother can succeed only when she starts her teaching as soon as her baby is in her womb. Actually, it starts even before that. A married woman starts planning to raise a family as soon as she is married, as it is the main reason for her marriage.

She discusses with her husband the right time to conceive, the right way to bring up their child and the right place for his welfare. They do not plan a family until they are themselves settled. In fact, they do not get married if they reckon that they will not be settled after their marriage. Consequently, most children are born soon after their parents are married. The father's relationship with the child starts then to a great extent, and the mother's to a much greater extent. It is a sort of theoretical relationship at this stage, but it is very important.

The parents want a healthy child, so they look after their own health. They want a well-behaved child so they cultivate their own behaviour. They want a well-protected child so they start saving for the future.

When the baby is born, the mother protects him from elements such as fire, water, accidents and diseases. By so doing, she strengthens the mother–child relationship and earns his sincerity, confidence and love. As he grows up, he meets more and more people and his mother guides him in forming a good relationship with them all. The good mother gives him only what is good for him, doing all she can and using all the resources available to mould him into a good future citizen, and to help him recognise, accept and practise good conduct and behaviour, and to reject unsocial or anti-social habits.

Here I must point out that all mothers are good, but many are misled and influenced by the world we live in. They prefer, and quite often they are constrained, to follow the easy way to bring up their children. Instead of training them to get used to healthy home-cooked foods, the mothers get them accustomed to unhealthy fast foods; instead of teaching them to read and write, which is time-consuming, the mothers buy them video games and films which keep them occupied for hours; instead of taking them to social functions and religious gatherings, the mothers take them to shopping precincts or let them play in unsupervised playgrounds. The result is negative as far as the mother–child relationship is concerned.

The mother spends less time with the child and instead of developing their relationship, they are weakening it. The child looks at the mother as a provider rather than as a carer and protector. While this relationship with his mother weakens, that with his toys, games and gadgets increases. He shows love towards her as long as she keeps providing what he wants (as opposed to what he needs). Since he spends more time with these objects than with her, and they are without feelings, he becomes less emotive and more insensible. He becomes more materialistic and less spiritual, more robotic and less human. Thus, the sentimental value in the human relationship is undermined.

The main ingredient of a human relationship is love, which takes many forms, often manifested collectively: for example, a mother is often a friend, a teacher, a nurse and a benefactor. A person's relationship with all these cannot be sustained without love. Without love a mother cannot raise a child; two friends cannot be lovers; a teacher cannot teach his pupils; a nurse cannot tend her patients; and a donor cannot help a recipient. One cannot perform a duty without love for it, and it is this love that is the binding force in any relationship – be it between a king and his subjects; between a human and an animal; between an animal and an object; or between an object and another object – be it formed consciously or unconsciously; be it permanent or temporary; be it predestined or spontaneous.

If we recognise this subtle, pervading love then peace will prevail globally. By not doing so we create enemies. For example, the terrorist does not realise the clothes he is wearing may have been manufactured by the very people he kills, or the food he eats may have been the product of his victims, or the people he wants to kill may be those who will look after him if he is wounded. Let us go a step further. He may be breathing the same air that has passed through the nostrils of those he wants to annihilate; or, the water he drinks may have been drawn from their blood and sweat; or again, the earth he treads on may have their footprints on it.

His ignorance blocks the power of his realisation. He does not even realise that the breeze that caresses his cheeks is the same that has stroked the cheeks of those he mistakenly judges to be his enemies. How can a person destroy those to whom he is related in one way or another? Yet he does, because he does not understand.

It is this lack of understanding that has sunk this world into turmoil. Is it possible to come out of it? I believe it is, but it will take time. We all know that the right education dispels ignorance. But are we promoting the right education? Not in my opinion, because modern technology shows us how to count to ten without teaching us the value of numbers zero to nine. In other words, we don't learn what is basic and most important.

Here is what I propose: let all the leaders of all the states put their heads together at a universal conference and come up with a formula whereby every single person in the world is guaranteed education. I believe there are enough resources around to do this. The next step is to compile texts on universal ethics and eti-quettes, which will be incorporated in all the examinations worldwide. This must be a compulsory subject – a subject that must be studied and practised by all. The study and practice will determine the student's results in any examination.

Let this be the basis of globalisation. I believe this is the missing link in the preparation for world peace. As it is in this day and age, this is what modern technology has left out. This is why globalisation, which must begin at home, is impossible; this is why members of the same family are in conflict with one another. The same applies to members of a society or citizens of a country.

Good human relationships, which will result from this preparation, will bring harmony, freedom and peace in the world, for the third or fourth generation from now. Right now we must all – parents, teachers, priests, politicians and peacekeepers – work together to achieve this end, instead of selfishly protecting or wanting to protect ourselves. It won't be easy, but it won't be impossible if we do not preoccupy ourselves with issues – which, of course, also need to be focussed on – such as poverty in different parts of the world, the detrimental forces of our environment, social erosion, the effects of wars, the recrudescence and birth of diseases.

This subject for the texts must be developed and designed to accommodate the different stages of the person's ability to assimilate its content and to practise it; and only the universally accepted practices must be identified. For example, a person must respect his elders. Each principle must be elaborated upon for the different stages of the examinations. For example, it is no good just to learn that it is the duty of a person to do good and be good. What *is* good must be clearly defined and the reasons for this principle must be logically explained at length. If it conflicts with logic, it is not acceptable.

For example, if a person believes 'Love thy neighbour as thyself', it is illogical for him to think that the neighbour must belong to the same class, colour or creed as him; but it is logical for him to think that the neighbour can be anybody whatever his class, colour or creed, and he must love all his neighbours without prejudice or preference. Therefore, a principle that has no logic in it cannot be universally accepted. The universally accepted good manners, principles and actions can only produce universally accepted good people in future generations.

Good people practise love and live in freedom, harmony and peace. Good people are noble and just. They do not – they cannot – indulge in unjust and ignoble practices. Let us make the whole world noble.

Noble people alone are capable of effecting and upholding good human relationships, the highest nature of which exists between one human being and another. A person also forms a relationship with an animal, but if he allows this to be stronger than that with a human being, he greatly damages his feelings towards other humans. A person's relationship with an object can also be allowed to exceed that with other human beings, and this again will damage his human feelings, only more so, as in the case of a person who loves money more than people. Unfortunately, we are not living in a world of only noble people. Therefore, some people have more love for animals than for their own kind. Others have more love for objects than for human beings. Consequently, our genuine human feelings are considerably weakened and we harbour hatred instead of love, greed instead of benevolence, egoism instead of philanthropy, and so on.

Besides the home and school, sociocultural societies play a key role in moulding the character and relationships of children. All these societies must have firm and universal rules, which have been conceived, composed and commended by the heads of all the countries at a world conference on human relationships. Every society must have at least one session each week. Every individual must become the member of one society and attend its sessions with his family at least forty times a year.

Only matters relating to ethics, etiquette and humanity must concern these societies. These subjects must be learnt and practised by all. The societies must be empowered to issue certificates of morality and recommendations for school admissions, travel abroad, jobs and this sort of thing, and they must have the right to organise activities such as sermons by eminent scholars and sages, and workshops on social problems like drug addiction, alcoholism, gambling and other evils gnawing at society.

Here I must point out that once the recommendations of the world conference are carried out, there will be very little cause to organise these workshops, because everyone will become a responsible person and an ideal individual. However, these workshops must be held from time to time to ensure that those evils never resurface.

These societies will definitely establish good human relationships since all the individuals will be governed by the same constructive, humanitarian and philanthropic curricula. A society may be annexed to a religious organisation provided that the religious teachings do not conflict with those of the society. The teachings of a true religion cannot possibly conflict with the universally approved humanitarian philosophy.

Of course, not all societies we have are sociocultural. Societies have other disciplines. Some we must take seriously, some less seriously, and some we must reject completely. For example, literary circles, which are now unfortunately dwindling in number, must be taken seriously; sports associations and fan clubs, which are now increasing in number, must be taken less seriously; while gambling clubs, which are also unfortunately increasing in number, must be rejected; whereas syndicates of criminals must be annihilated. We have become victims of societies that do not help much to improve the welfare of the human race. We must, therefore, take a fresh and concerned look at the societies around us and do something positive and quick to change their image. I believe that all societies approved and registered according to law must first and foremost exercise the universally accepted ethics, etiquette and moral values.

Though I am not a leader of any state, I would like a few of my suggestions to be examined, and, if universally approved, implemented in this philosophy.

1. Every individual is a human being and must be treated as such.

2. It is the sacred duty of all parents, societies and governments to inculcate good conduct and manners in their children and to ennoble them.

3. Every individual must learn and practise good manners. This can be achieved through parents, schools and societies. Therefore, the study and practice of good conduct and manners must be included in the school curriculum, in the society's agenda and in the parents' duties.

4. Government officials must supervise the work of these

teachers; that is, the schools, the societies and the parents.

5. Every individual must be taught the positivistic and constructive qualities in life along with the negativistic and destructive aspects of it. For example, he must know and practise love, but he must also know what hatred is and why he must reject it.

6. Every individual must learn and practise these positivistic and constructive aspects at all stages of their life, from infancy to old age. I care to mention a few: piety, love, charity, altruism, honesty, integrity, non-violence, brotherhood, respect, reverence, hospitality, compassion and sincerity.

7. Colour, class or creed must not interfere with, impede or lower the dignity, freedom, peace, progress and happiness of the individual.

8. Every individual must renounce and reject such negativistic attitudes and behaviour as hatred, anger, pride, selfishness, brutality, injustice, covetousness, greed, licentiousness, lust, irreligion, oppression, partiality, impatience and all other bad manners.

9. Every individual must value and respect his own and others' possessions.

10. Every individual must exercise cleanliness and protect the environment.

11. Every individual must be employed in a job and must not press for an excessive and loss-making salary. He must also do a fair day's work.

12. No individual must harbour sloth and laziness.

13. Every individual must become a member of an approved society that works for the advancement of mankind.

14. Every individual must embrace truth and reject untruth and superstitions.

15. Every individual must acquire a good and righteous education.

16. Education on conduct, ethics, etiquette and integrity must be made compulsory.

17. Discrimination must be outlawed in all the countries of the world.

18. Poverty must be wiped out so that its consequences will cease to exist.

19. The government must ensure the protection of freedom for all.

20. Education, health and welfare services must be free and accessible to every individual.

I am certain that there are more persons more qualified than me. They can contribute a lot more towards the advancement of mankind. They can add to or modify my suggestions. Their efforts to make the world a better place for future generations will be invaluable. I appeal to these intelligent and godly people to work together and conceive a universally accepted programme on human behaviour that will be compulsory in all school curricula. This will consequently motivate parents and societies to ensure that their children learn the subject, practise it and later teach their own children.

The human relationships that emerge will only promote harmony and happiness in the world. Where there is harmony there is peace and freedom. *Harmony! Peace! Freedom! Happiness!* What a beautiful world it will be! If modern technology complemented this world, the ideal situation would have been achieved. Alas! Technology has left the cradle of harmony, peace, freedom and happiness behind to nest in the bed of stress, strife and selfishness. The true feelings of human relationships are lost in the whirlpool of materialism where love is replaced by hatred; humbleness by power; happiness by misery; and integrity by shamelessness.

When I come across people who resent, quite often with verbal abuse or physical violence, the sound and constructive advice about their wrong deeds, words and ways of life, I wonder firstly, what has happened to human relationships, and secondly, why one bothers to advise the wrongdoers. Is it not better to let a sleeping dog lie? But then, the wrongdoers almost always infect a good society. Shall we, therefore, live in fear of the wrongdoers or shall we be brave enough to correct them at the expense of being verbally abused, threatened or physically beaten up?

If we are afraid, and most of us are nowadays, then there is little we can do to improve human relationships. To win the wrongdoers over to our side we need to learn the technique of how to approach them – 'the approach technique'.

How to approach someone who may be angry, humiliated, ill, grieving, violent, ill-mannered, uneducated, superstitious, fanatical, mentally disturbed or just fed up with life; who may be young, middle-aged, old, strong, weak, rich, poor, black, white, hungry, overweight or just looked down upon; who may be a prince or a pauper, a saint or a sinner, a carer or a criminal, a lord or a layperson; or just a woman or a whore, is not learnt over-night. It is an intrinsic build-up in the proper upbringing of an ideal individual.

Of course, even if every individual were raised properly there would still be a few wrongdoers, but it would be easy to approach them and give them sound advice without any risk of adverse and negativistic reaction. To approach a well-bred individual for his lapse (for erring is human) should be an intuitive duty of man. Sadly, though, our veritable instincts are hiding behind a purdah of conceit, resentment and apathy. Wrongdoers have far outnum-bered philanthropists. But I do not believe that we must join the wrongdoers if we cannot beat them. We must relentlessly fight them until they join us. Then we shall be able to create an ideal world to live in. But we cannot succeed unless we have the support of and enforcement from the government, which must be the most powerful weapon in our struggle. That is why a government must make it compulsory for everyone to learn and practise good behaviour and undertake only those activities that promote a utopian society.

Culture

Statement

One of the main reasons for wars and conflicts within a state is the fact that people identify themselves with their culture first, and not with their country.

Inquiry

If they had put their country first, do you think there would have been no conflicts?

Statement

When did I say that? I said the above is one of the *main* reasons. Sometimes I believe it is *the* main reason.

Inquiry

Your other reasons?

Statement

Well, there is lust for power, greed for material possessions, politics, misinterpretation and/or misunderstanding of religion, or terrorism perpetrated by brainwashed fanatical groups, who are so ignorant that they don't know what they really believe in or what they really want.

Inquiry

All right! But how can culture be the main reason for conflicts in a country?

Statement

Culture divides people when they give it more importance than their country. Take the example of a multicultural state. It can exist peacefully as long as the people of this state do not identify their sectarian and distinct culture with the country. If they do, the country will be split into as many parts as the number of cultural groups each wanting to impose on the others. This is so obvious in all multicultural countries nowadays. Once the country is divided, each division – that is, each ethnic group – wants to rule over the whole country. Since each group has different beliefs and ways of life that they want to prevail, conflicts become inevitable.

Inquiry

But the same can be said of politics or religion or terrorist groups.

Statement

It seems so but I think it should not be so. Politics, genuine politics, must be served by true politicians whose duty is, among others, to unite the people. True politicians must be learned, just, impartial, patriotic, upright, uncorrupted and incorruptible, honest and competent. They must be devoted to the welfare of their people and their country. They must be humble without being cowardly. They must be firm without being domineering. They must be exemplary. Unfortunately, very few genuine politicians are born nowadays. Most politicians play one ethnic group against another for their own selfish gains. Culture is exploited and conflicts start. People following a culture are quite sensible but also quite sensitive and gullible; hence they are the politicians' butts. But it is the culture that is the root cause of any conflict that ensues.

On the other hand, terrorists are insensible and often mindless people whose fanatical beliefs brainwash them into killing others and creating a conflicting situation in a country. The terrorists may not even belong to the country they attack and destroy; therefore, they are cruel and merciless.

Inquiry

What about religion?

Statement

Sadly, in a country ravaged by wars and conflicts, religion does not exist – the religion of humanity and truth, that is. I believe true religion can only generate and propagate love, not war. However, very few people practise true religion, hence war becomes inevitable.

Inquiry

Do you really believe that a country without internal conflicts is possible?

Statement

Absolutely. A series of actions needs to be taken before it becomes possible. It is paramount that the attitude and mentality of people be changed for the better to allow the implementation of all other actions.

Inquiry

What's wrong with people's attitudes and mentality?

Statement

First and foremost, we have – most of us, anyway – become materialistic. Materialism means distancing ourselves from spirituality.

Inquiry

There's nothing wrong if a person is materialistic.

Statement

There is. Let's probe the world of materialists. What do materialists want? First and foremost, they want money so they can accumulate tangible possessions such as properties, cars, luxurious furniture and so on. They want plenty of money to spend on other wants which they don't necessarily need; for example, frequent visits to restaurants, unnecessary clothes and other wear, gambling, alcohol and cigarettes, holidays, expensive toys for their children and parties.

Before they have all these they are all so busy accumulating money by fair and often foul means that they have no time for anything else that is important, such as social and charitable activities, spiritual upliftment and God. When they have all they want they are so engrossed in enjoying their acquisitions that they still have no time for anything else. They tend to forget they have their familial, social, patriotic, religious and spiritual duties to perform. They also keep changing what they have for the sake of keeping up with or outdoing their own kind. They become greedy, jealous and selfish.

Inquiry

Are you saying that all materialists are greedy, jealous and selfish?

Statement

No. Fortunately, they are all humans. Human beings are born with human instincts such as philanthropy, spirituality, humanitarianism, kindness, humility, the desire to live in a society, and other righteous qualities that can never be completely overridden by materialism. However, such human instincts are unfortunately acknowledged and observed by very few people nowadays. Most of us are individualistic. This is bad for our country. We must change our mentality and attitude and create an awareness of unity. We can achieve it if we follow our instincts.

We must unite and establish a common culture, which will be practised by all in a multiracial and multicultural country. The deviation from our true instincts and adoption of materialism is stopping us from achieving this goal; that is, a common culture, a national culture: a common national culture.

Inquiry

Didn't you say culture divides? Then why establish a culture?

Statement

Yes. I was referring to the way it is exploited at present in countries not having a national culture and in countries where the national culture is not followed earnestly and equitably. A common culture founded on national interests, accepted and practised by one and all, does not stand above the country. It is at one with her. The two being one means that no division is created.

Inquiry

What are the policies of such a culture and how can they be implemented?

Statement

First, we must change our attitude and mentality. We must stop being individualists. We must stop being materialists. We must stop being sectarians. We must stop being separatists. We must stop being unpatriotic.

We must firmly and loyally believe in 'one nation, one people'. We must observe all the principles that are beneficial to one and all, and which promote national welfare. We must promote the physical, social and spiritual good of every sentient being. Our conduct towards all should be guided by love, righteousness and justice. We must reject untruth and embrace truth. We must uphold knowledge and reject nescience.

We must cultivate patience, love, forgiveness, humbleness, morality, calm, spirituality and nobility. We must all belong to a society based on these principles. Let this be our true culture. The politics of such a culture can be implemented if our educational institutions, societies and the state work together with strict discipline. Under the umbrella of this culture no one will behave in an uncivilised manner.

There will be no cause for riots, civil disobedience or hooliganism. Freedom and peace will reign, and above all, unity. All ugly incidents will automatically cease. Everyone will be a law-abiding citizen. There will be no corruption and no dirty politics.

Inquiry

Where will be the place for individual freedom to practise one's own religion and perform one's rituals and observance?

Statement

Upholding our national culture will be our religion, but individuals shall be free to conduct their rituals and rights in their own way in the privacy of their own homes, churches, mosques and temples. These should not interfere or conflict with the national religion. As a matter of fact, these will be respected by the noble citizens of the country, once their attitude and mentality change. The culture of the individual will never override the national culture. Our national culture can become an international culture if all the countries adopt the same principles.

Inquiry

Do you think it is possible to adapt to these principles?

Statement

Yes. It seems impossible because there is hypocrisy in our attitude and mentality.

Inquiry

How do you come to this conclusion?

Statement

Let me refer to a public lecture I had the privilege to attend. It was entitled 'The Literature of Indo-Fijian Diaspora'. Many points were raised, the most sensitive of which concerned conflicts between the indigenous Fijians and the Indo-Fijians, each group claiming the right to Fiji's sovereignty. I believe this is less important than what all of them want and what they really are. What they really want is peace and freedom and the prosperity of Fiji.

They are really human beings who have together moulded the present state of the country. Together they can work and live happily. *This* is important. Issues which split the nation and create conflicts are not important. Often we think about, talk about and do what contradicts our true and treasured wishes. Otherwise, why must two or more groups who have basically the same goal in life destroy it by unwanted and violent conflicts?

We cannot pretend that communal, and not national, culture is not one of the main reasons for these conflicts. Communalism must, therefore, be excluded from all the activities concerning public interest and national welfare.

Inquiry

It is a bit confusing, isn't it? You say, if I am not mistaken, that international culture alone will change people's attitudes and mentality, and at the same time, you insist that only our changed attitude and mentality can establish an international culture. It is like asking which came first, the egg or the chicken, isn't it?

Statement

It may seem confusing at first. It is not easy to change a wide-spread and deep-rooted attitude and mentality. It will be easier for us to raise a new breed of people with attitude and mentality quite different from ours. We must be honest and earnest. A smoker can tell non-smokers that smoking is bad. An alcoholic can tell teetotallers that drinking is bad. A gambler can tell non-gamblers that gambling is bad.

In the same way we can tell the new generation from its very birth that our attitude and mentality are bad, and teach them a good attitude and mentality. Of course we shall create a gap between our generation and the new one. Maybe this is necessary. It will stop the fire of our generation from engulfing the new crops of the future generation. If you want to stop a fire from spreading, create an empty space in its path. The fire will die but the new generation beyond the empty space will flourish.

Inquiry

Do you think that global culture will not work out for our generation?

Statement

Global culture will work out for our generation if we stop being hypocrites. The truth is, we want a global culture but we are not prepared to relinquish the materialism that dominates our lives. We are stubborn and do not want to accept it. We are greedy and egoistic and we do not want to accept it. We harbour many enemies such as anger, impatience, unforgiveness, violence and the like and we do not want to accept it. We have strayed from spirituality and we do not want to accept it. We prefer indolence to diligence and we do not want to accept it. We do many wrongs and we do not want to accept it. How, then, can a global culture aiming to bring peace, harmony, freedom, happiness and welfare for all, work out for our generation? It won't.

Inquiry

Hence you believe we must strive towards a global culture for the future generation?

Statement

Absolutely. It has become imperative now to seriously consider the establishment of a global culture for the future generations. Global culture cannot exist as long as religious groups publicly display their strength in numbers and in any other manner. This display becomes a challenge and a threat to other groups who also want to display their strength.

A violent competition ensues. These groups then distance themselves from one another. They also create an unfriendly gap among themselves. Tension arises. When this gets beyond control then conflicts start. Such conflicts are quite common nowadays, and are on the increase. We have caused them and we don't want to accept it.

That is why a global culture will not work for us. Therefore, it is our duty to prevent our disease from spreading to the new generations, and we can do it only by establishing a global culture that will bring harmony and unity instead of distance and conflicts among groups of people of different religions. Global culture will also fail if it is not incorporated in the curricula of all academic examinations.

It must be a compulsory subject to learn and to practise at home, at school and in society. The government must ensure this. Global culture must be governed by many rules, regulations and ways of life. Here I suggest the following twenty-three tenets, to which many more can be added, and which can become the foundation on which global culture will stand.

1. Every individual must regard humanity as sacred and must promote its welfare.

2. All human beings are equal and it is the duty of every individual to safeguard this equality.

3. Every individual must respect and protect his fundamental rights and the rights of others.

4. Every individual must practise brotherhood and friendship.

5. Every individual must promote love and discard hatred.

6. Every individual must endeavour to become a law-abiding citizen.

7. Every individual must attend school, and it is the duty of every government to provide its citizens with proper education.

8. Every student must learn and practise global culture.

9. Global culture must be included in the curricula of all examinations, and it must be a compulsory subject.

10. Every individual must be a member of a registered society qualified to issue certificates of morality and good conduct.

11. All applications for jobs, schools and so on must be supported by certificates of morality.

12. It must be the legal duty of parents to raise their children with discipline in conformity with the guidelines laid down by an agreed global culture.

13. Code of conduct and behaviour approved by global culture must be observed by all individuals.

14. Violence against any individual must be severely punished.

15. Swear words and vulgar language must not be used by anybody. Offenders must be punished without prejudice.

16. Sexual discrimination must be wiped out.

17. There must be equal opportunity for men and women in the areas in which they are both participating.

18. It is the duty of each individual to respect and care for his parents.

19. Every individual must be polite and chivalrous at all times.

20. Every individual must learn to control anger, impatience, jealousy, greed, extravagance and other undesirable characteristics. Special schools must be provided for this education.

21. Every individual must exercise philanthropy.

22. Injustice and corruption must be wiped out.

23. Individuals must help and not hinder each other.

Inquiry

All you say sounds good, but I detect a contradiction in your statement. Children normally copy what their parents do. Therefore, it follows that the parents must change first. Doesn't it? But then you state that the parents are hypocrites and stubborn and they won't change. How can they raise children who will be different from them?

Statement

I must admit that I have been a bit crafty. Let me tell you what happened to X who was drinking excessively, smoking about twenty cigarettes a day, gambling every day and flirting with women all the time. He had a good business managed by a sincere friend; so X could afford to pursue his bad habits although he was fed up with them. He told me he just could not give up any of his bad habits but he wanted to get out of the mess they were dragging him into.

I advised him not to give up any of his bad habits, but at the same time, just for one year, to practise just one good habit, and that was to join a religio-social group and attend its two-hourly once-weekly sessions. Do you know what happened after he listened to me? After six months his bad habits started to crumble and he was taking a keen interest in his one good habit.

After a year all his bad habits vanished and he became the most active and devoted member of the religio-social group. He did not even realise how it happened, when it happened or how easily it happened. Good always triumphs over evil. If our motives are good, our hypocrisy and our obstinacy will disappear without our knowledge of how, when, and how easily it happens. There cannot be a better motive than creating a peaceful and blissful world for our progeny.

Inquiry

You have indeed been crafty. But why did you reveal this secret?

Statement

Sooner or later people would have found out. But that is not important. It is important that we understand why we need to change our attitude. It is important that we try to change it. As we say: 'Nothing ventured, nothing gained.' What does it matter if what we want for our own children inspires us to change our attitude and mentality? It is also better that we change these voluntarily rather than subconsciously, because we appreciate more what we willingly, knowingly and purposely do. We must also be resolute in achieving our purpose. Whatever happens to us, let us build for the coming generation a world that they will be proud to live in. They will also be proud of us for bringing them into a stress-free world of peace, freedom, harmony, bliss and prosperity, in a world where love, humanity, justice, meritocratic principles and piety will prevail.

Violence

Violence is probably the most prevalent destructive force in the world in which we live. It is also the fastest growing undesirable aspect of our life. Ironically, we all practise it, even those who campaign against it. We display it verbally, physically and mentally, sometimes unconsciously and often consciously, directing it towards ourselves or towards others, secretly or openly, and in varying degrees. The most vulnerable recipients of violence are women and children who cannot protect and defend themselves as effectively as men do. The most notorious dispensers of violence are those men who are mindless and cruel and who think it is their divine right to exercise it.

It is not only at home that violence erupts but also in societies, on the streets, in offices; and at national and international levels. It cannot be denied that violence has reached an alarming height globally in whatever field we care to mention: and whatever action we take to suppress it, it is on the increase. This demonstrates our failure to tackle it. Therefore, we have to look afresh at our strategy. For this, we have to find out where we have gone wrong. It is easy if we stop being stubborn in pretending that we are not wrong, and in being confident that we will succeed in our present handling of violence.

Before the situation deteriorates further and goes beyond our control, if it is not already, let me give my contribution towards a solution. First, I have to compare very briefly two ages in the history of mankind: the age when violence was non-existent and our present age when violence is rife.

I have heard of and I believe that there was a time when all men and women were noble. They were all pious and believed in one God. They used to get up early and never started their day without performing their prayers and reminding themselves of the virtues they were born with and promising to uphold them. They were simple, happy and peaceful people who were satisfied with whatever God had given them: the gift of good health, soundness of intellect, the profundity of compassion, the purity of love and the strength to practise and maintain truth, justice, humanity, altruism and brotherhood. They lived in peace and harmony, freedom and security, honesty and happiness, equality and prosperity.

They had great respect, admiration and consideration for one another and one another's values. They were blessed with judgement and understanding. Their days were spent working diligently and their evenings in prayer, followed by meals and social gatherings where they would listen to discourses by men of wisdom, and which were attended by adults and children alike; their nights in peaceful sleep. They were people of great moral and religious principles based on Divine Laws and Truth, living in the plenitude of peace, bliss and freedom. Their well-balanced diet and diligence kept them mentally and physically healthy.

There was no room for violence in that age. There could not have been as there was no cause for it. In contrast, our modern age is acutely infested with the vermin of violence that gnaws at our freedom, peace and happiness. These rapacious and merciless microbes have infiltrated every aspect of our life. We witness children's violence towards other children; parents' violence towards their children and vice versa; husbands' violence towards their wives and vice versa; police violence towards criminals and vice versa; employers' violence towards employees and vice versa; suppliers' violence towards customers and vice versa; rich people's violence towards poor people and vice versa; the rulers' violence towards their subjects and vice versa; the peacekeepers' violence towards rebels and vice versa; one society's violence towards another and vice versa; the whites' violence towards the blacks and vice versa; one family's violence towards another and vice versa; the captor's violence towards the captives and vice versa; and so on and so forth.

Most of us exercise violence at some stage in our lives in one way or another, but none of us wishes to be a *victim* of violence. We all hate violence because it hurts, whether it is verbal, physical or mental. As a matter of fact, verbal and mental violence can hurt just as much, if not more than, physical violence. We are living in a violent world, and therefore we must not pretend that all is well in it and let indifference grow on us.

The two ages are worlds apart. How did it happen? How did heaven turn into hell? Stagnant water gets polluted more easily than the flowing river. People became complacent with God's gifts and started to stagnate instead of flowing to the ocean of divinity and purity. In that stagnation, microbes of degeneration and regression took root and spread in all directions of our life.

From this stage emerged lust, greed, anger, frustration, immorality, illusion, delusions of grandeur, a power struggle and violence. Love for one another lost its meaning. Hatred for one another developed. We started killing one another.

When killing becomes a matter of course for a human being, he kills an animal or another human with the same ease and heartlessness. Killing is one of the many effects of violence. The killer and abetter are both guilty of killing. As long as killings continue, there will be no lasting peace, as it has proved in many countries. It is ironical that men kill even (or especially?) on occasions which are holy, as when they celebrate the birth of a saint or a messiah. Over two-thirds of the world's population are, therefore, responsible for the killings of millions of animals during these occasions.

Does it not follow that two-thirds of the world are violent? How, then, can we stamp out violence? We must bring back the era when peace, freedom and love reigned. To do that, it is imperative that we clearly understand and recognise that we are human beings gifted with intelligence and capable of differentiating between right and wrong, between good and bad, between justice and injustice, between morality and immorality, between love and hatred, between the beauty of peace and the ugliness of war, but above all, between ourselves and animals.

Other species are not as intelligent as human beings and are, therefore, inferior and incapable of achieving what we have and can. We are quite capable of creating a peaceful world for ourselves. It is so simple. We do not have to do anything in particular before we start doing something. We simply have to stop doing a series of things, and peace will be established by itself; and once this is achieved, we can plan what we have to 'do'.

Here are the things we have to stop:

1. Harbouring hatred in our hearts and ill-will in our minds.

2. Giving in to qualities such as anger, impatience, malice, jealousy, violence, cruelty, covetousness, thievery and other evils that are harmful to us.

3. Indulging in materialism.

4. Believing in the teachings of the wrong scriptures.

5. Supporting a regime for selfish gains.

6. Practising illogical rituals and accepting superstitious and false beliefs.

7. Tolerating and encouraging injustices, corruption and partiality.

8. Conducting immoral practices.

9. Practising bad manners.

10. Rejecting truth and logic.

Suppose we have stopped all these, what are we left with? A heart replete with love, a mind replete with peace and a life replete with happiness; all of these due only to cessation of actions. We have accomplished half of our goal. We have already created the era when peace, freedom and love reign. We now need to accomplish the other half of our goal.

Becoming complacent and remaining stagnant here will be fatal as it has proved in the past. We must build upon what we have achieved. We can do that now, by taking action.

Where do we start? Ideally we must start with the prospective parents. They must learn the science of setting up a peaceful home and of raising children who will grow up with excellence in manners and conduct. To learn this science they must look for gurus. Their parents, their society, the schools, people with wisdom and the right scriptures are worthy gurus.

The prospective parents must have time to attend their lectures. If they give up the addictions they are indulging in, they will find plenty of time in their lives. These addictions include compulsive viewing of soap operas, indulgence in unnecessary conversations, extravagant time-consuming shopping, flirtatious outings, love for bed and undertaking the wrong activities. These are all counterproductive and harmful. For example, those who are obsessed with soap operas identify themselves with the characters in them. They copy their lifestyle and behave like them. They do not accept the fact that the characters and their behaviour are not true to life. The soap operas that have won over their viewers are full of intrigues, spiteful characters and unreal situations. It is these that mesmerise the viewers.

In a compelling soap opera, there is generally only one good character who is surrounded by many bad characters trying to make the good one's life miserable. Soap operas with only pleasant and good characters attract fewer viewers. Unfortunately, the virtues of the good character are rarely copied. The vulgarisms and vulgarities are easily copied. As a result, most of us have become like the characters in the compelling soap operas: hateful, spiteful, gossipy, violent, conceited, vulgar and unreasonable.

All the other addictions cause harm in like manner and in some other ways. They are destructive forces which must be stamped out. If we do that, we shall all have plenty of time for constructive activities. The prospective parents will benefit most if they learn from the gurus how to create an atmosphere of love, peace and rectitude in each home.

They will learn how to control anger and uphold healthy dialogues, thus avoiding any form of argument leading to violence. They will learn to establish long and lasting relation-ships with one another and to treat every member of the family with dignity, respect and love. They will inculcate their own good conduct into their children. It is said that children are like kneaded clay that can be moulded into any shape. It is true that children take after their parents. If the parents are good, their children will be good. In fact, all children must excel over their parents, even marginally, otherwise there is no progress in the world.

The children must learn everything from their parents right from birth. Their learning will be strengthened as they grow, through societies and schools, and through the learned people to whom their parents will introduce them. Their strength will be in their patience, non-violence, humbleness, philanthropy, spirituality, moral integrity, intelligence, nobility and justice. Children of this calibre will always resort to reason and not to violence, at home, at school and in society. They will be the ones who will one day create a wonderful world to live in, for themselves and for the generations after them – a world without violence.

Discipline

D iscipline is a vital and integral part of any aspect of life and nature. It is the essence of success. Chaos rules where it is lacking or inadequate. Where chaos rules disintegration results. Even disintegration has to follow the law of discipline whether it takes place rapidly or gradually. If a log is allowed to rot, it will take a long time but the process of rotting must follow a set pattern. If the log is burnt, it will take a short time but it will still follow a set pattern. The decay will follow the wood and not vice versa. The ashes will follow the ember and not vice versa, because the law of discipline controls these processes.

I believe, and I am sure many will support my belief, that a disciplined child is more likely to succeed in life than an undisciplined one; that a disciplined society is more peaceful and prosperous than an undisciplined one; that a disciplined school gives better results than an undisciplined one; that a disciplined state is more stable and progressive than an undisciplined one. An army with the highest level of discipline is feared by an enemy force however big this is, simply because the disciplined army is difficult to rout.

Let us for a moment analogise this with present day life. Most of us have some very powerful enemies, such as a lust for power and wealth, submission to conceit and pride, addiction to gambling and vice, obsession with luxury and extravagance. It is obvious that if we do not discipline our desires, reasoning faculties and willpower, we are likely to be doomed. With our disciplined and powerful army, we can rout our enemies before it is too late. It will be too late if we allow our defence to ignore or neglect discipline, while simultaneously allowing our enemies to exercise discipline.

Our life is not so worthless that we allow it to be enslaved by our merciless enemies. We must prepare ourselves to fight our enemies. We must bring discipline into our lives. It must be ingrained in us from the moment of birth. A mother trains her baby when to expect to be changed, fed and nestled in her cosy lap. The baby learns to recognise the times for these needs. He learns not to cry unnecessarily for them. He learns to be patient and compromising. Step by step she educates him in how to associate discipline with time, people and place. For example, he learns when and where to sleep; when and where to play with his toys; when, where and how to have his meals; what and whom to listen to; how and whom to obey; where and how to keep his toys and clothes; how and when to brush his teeth and so on. Without this education, the child grows up to be an ill-behaved and undisciplined person.

Two factors are necessary to teach discipline. First, the teacher must herself be a disciplined person. Secondly, the teacher must herself understand the relation of time, people and place to discipline. Time is important in our lives. We cannot waste it. Without discipline, it is wasted. For example, if the instruments in an operating theatre are not kept in an orderly way, looking for them will waste time and can be fatal for the person undergoing an operation. Anyone can imagine what will happen to an army on the battleground if the weapons and ammunition are not in order. Similarly, if we do not bring discipline into our lives, we will encounter disastrous results in whatever we venture to do.

We must have discipline in every aspect of our lives. We need to organise our lives to accommodate it. We can do it with ease if only we have the will. The problem is, we take time for granted too often except when time imposes on us. When we have a train or a plane to catch, we make sure we reach the station or the airport on time. When we have an interview for a job, we are on time. When we have to sit for an examination, we are on time. Why, then, do we want to start our work five minutes late and leave the place of work five minutes early? Why, then, do we start a meeting late and let it go on beyond its closing time? Why don't we have our meals on time? Why don't we get up on time for our prayers? Why don't we leave our home early for the vital things in life instead of starting late and rushing? Why do we make our lives chaotic?

I believe that if we bring discipline into our lives we can succeed in our reasonably physical, mental, spiritual and moral aspirations. In fact, all our activities will become automatic and simple. The sun is able to complete effortlessly its daily revolution because it always starts on time. If we follow the example of the sun we too can effortlessly complete our day's work on time, thus avoiding rush and stress. It follows that a lack of discipline in our lives is one of the major reasons for our stress, which evidently is the cause of so many illnesses and so much unhappiness, impatience and anger.

Indiscipline is also the cause of many accidents. I was once stopped by police on a motorway in England because I had driven for a long distance in the middle lane without a valid reason. I was asked if I knew about lane discipline. I knew it but I was not conforming to it. Very politely, the police officer advised me to do so. We all know that many accidents are caused by drivers not observing lane discipline, though they know about it and how much easier and safer it is to obey it.

Many of us just do not care. Whether consciously or unconsciously, we do not care about so many important things in our lives: what we say, what we do, what we eat, how we behave, what our humanitarian duties are, what happens to others if the code of moral, religious and social conduct is ignored, all because we do not appreciate the values of discipline. We forget that every aspect of our lives has lane discipline and if we do not conform to it, our lives will be full of accidents.

However, in many cases in our lives, we all exercise discipline because we know its importance. When we ignore this knowledge, we are required by law to apply it. This need not be so if we are raised with strict discipline right from birth. The truth is, we do not raise our children with strict discipline, which is vital for the advancement of mankind. For example, we know that littering is hazardous for our health and the environment and yet we go on littering our country, but when a law against littering is strictly enforced, we observe it.

Why can't we do this voluntarily since we are aware of the consequences of littering? It is sad that because we have become irresponsible people, strict discipline enforced by law is the only way to educate us on a subject so easy to learn and act upon.

Being irresponsible, we raise undisciplined children, hence we create undesirable situations. It is shameful to watch hooligans who are barely five years old. I have witnessed children of eight years beating their mothers, and ten-year-olds running away from home. I have seen young children playing in the parks at night. I have heard young children using vulgar language and terrorising old people. I have seen them drinking alcohol and smoking.

No wonder we read about young girls engaging in drug-taking and prostitution! I place the blame primarily on irresponsible parents because I believe children grow up in the way they are trained and disciplined. If all children are disciplined from birth, they will have like companions and there will be no undisciplined children to influence others. So, a collective effort from all parents to raise well-mannered children is required.

Their effort will then be consolidated by social and educational institutions. The effort must be combined and continuous until the 'children' become responsible persons. The children will then take over the role of their parents, while schools and societies must never relinquish *their* role.

Because we are living in an age of materialism and our children are automatically following us, a tremendous amount of sacrifice is required by the contemporary parents if they prefer disciplined children. The parents must discipline themselves first. They will have to relinquish many habits that have grown on them. Initially, they must break away from some of the transient pleasures of the material world and adopt some of the real joys of the spiritual world. For example, they must spend less time in front of the television and more time with their children and elders. They must make it a habit to sit with the family and have meals together. They must shorten their time in the pubs and spend more time at home with their families. They must take their children with them wherever they go, especially when they are attending social functions. They must supervise their children all the time. They must teach them their devotional duties. These

exercises are within their reach and means, hence the sacrifices are minimal and easy to carry out.

Discipline in our lives, our society, our government and in our world negates the degenerating effect of any transient progress we have achieved without discipline. It therefore behoves every individual to promote and improve discipline. This is also necessary for the survival of the human race. We cannot deny that we have survived until this day because of discipline, among other reasons. Chaos in all departments of our life would have destroyed us if discipline were ignored. I care to mention a few examples to support my statement.

Many civilisations have disappeared due to the decay of discipline. Many governments have failed due to the decline in discipline. Events like the Olympic Games and religious celebrations would not have survived without discipline. Local, national and international organisations and societies cannot function without discipline. No place of worship, education and legislation can exist without discipline. A world without discipline is inconceivable.

'Womanitarianism'

I am curious to know why in this day and age women have failed to take their rightful place in society; why they still allow themselves to be influenced by prejudicial rules and regulations, moral convictions and culture established by men and not by divine law; and why they do not become well-versed in religious matters and occupy the highest ranks in religious organisations. Why do women still follow the advice of men who have failed to establish global peace, harmony and freedom?

Only now, people are talking about global culture, which cannot be secured without the full participation of women who are ready to impose their divine rights. But what are these divine rights?

To understand, recognise and exercise their divine rights, I believe women must know not only who they are but also *what* they are. God did not create women only for procreation but also for creation. Being completely impartial, He endowed them with many qualities equal to men, many qualities inferior to men's and many qualities superior to men's, so that universally they are equal to men and can share equal responsibility in working for the advancement of mankind. Thus, men and women can occupy their respective places in society without being inferior or superior one to the other.

Certain ways in which men and women were equal have changed through the ages so that they have now lost their sense of equality. For example, men and women were equally humble at one time. Generally speaking, through their arrogance and probably through pride in their physical strength, men have become less humble. Women have remained the same and yet it seems they have become more humble. This is only an illusion. If we remove the arrogance and the pride, both men and women will again become equal in humbleness. But in today's world it is neither easy to remove the deep-rooted arrogance and pride from men nor eliminate the illusion.

The same can be said of patience, a virtue men and women once shared equally. The difference in its inequality is probably due to the responsibilities attached to them. Men were responsible for the provision of the needs in the house, women for the home. As materialism started to creep into society men wanted to meet their needs quickly rather than patiently; women did it the other way round. For example, women had to, and they still have to, bring up their children with love. This requires a lot of patience. Men needed money and they still do. For this they have to work hard. No one likes work more than money. Love for the family is a lot more passionate than love of work. While women cherished their patience, men neglected theirs.

Many other unequal qualities in men and women have similarly been identified. Sadly, their current face value is imagined to be real. Qualities like these, though superficially acknowledged, give women an advantage over men, because they are good qualities. However, there *are* other qualities that are God-given and that men wrongly believe have given them an advantage over women in certain areas, but they do not give men the overall superiority they tend to exercise. Women are in no way disadvantaged by their femininity. On the contrary, they deserve respect, love and admiration, because they are very important persons.

They are the substratum of creation. The human race cannot exist without them. For this alone, they are worthy of glorification. But they are also the embodiment of beauty and charm, not only in their physical image but also in their mental, spiritual and divine strength. This strength is displayed in the love they have for their children, families, societies and states, in the way they care for these, in their forgiving nature, in their charismatic charity.

I was once fascinated by a joke someone told me. A boy professed that he loved his mother more than his father. When asked why, he replied that his father had dumped him in a pit and it was his mother who took him out of it. Upon deep reflection I realised it was not really a joke. Whether clumsily, purposely, consciously, pleasantly, pleasurably, lovingly or dutifully, the father does occasion the formation of a zygote. The mother nurtures it in her womb.

For around nine months when the zygote undergoes a series

of changes and develops into an embryo, the mother cares for it, protects it, feeds it and ensures its good health before bringing it into this world. The love and devotion with which she does all this is extraordinary. Besides this monumental sacrifice, she does not neglect her other duties of looking after herself, her husband, her household, her social affairs, her contribution to the welfare of the state and her devotional and spiritual rites.

She makes sure she is healthy so that the embryo develops healthily. She makes sure that the environment in which she will bring up her offspring is salubrious. She makes sure the child's world is a safe and peaceful place. She makes sure she has created a loving family for the child. Of course, the understanding, loving and caring husband must support all her endeavours to reach her goal, otherwise she may not succeed. Herein lies the importance of the equality of men and women. We think it is a joke and laugh, but it is not a joke at all. The father does not 'dump' the boy. He places him in a very protected environment. He does it with a very calculated objective. The mother does not take the boy out of the 'pit' but keeps him away from dangers, in her womb until he is born. The boy is naturally more attached to the mother, and, therefore, he loves her more, but the love becomes well balanced as he grows and comprehends the equality of his parents' love and understands that both his parents are responsible for his upbringing. Man plays his role, woman hers.

Neither the woman's role nor the man's ends here. They are both equal though their roles are different. The woman has a mammoth task to accomplish in moulding the life of the child, and she can succeed with ease and panache if the man does not stop providing her with the means for her task. These means are both tangible and intangible. The woman requires a house wherein she creates her home; the man provides her with it. She needs money; he provides her with it. She needs comfort and he provides her with it. She needs his understanding, moral support and love, and he obliges. She needs time to rest; he ensures she gets it.

I have outlined a mother's role in the chapter 'Human Relationships'. It is obvious that woman symbolises sacrifice, affection, devotion and friendship. She is an ocean of love and forgiveness. She is the queen of responsibility. She is the light that guides all the members of her family. She always tries her best to create an appropriate climate for the physical, mental and spiritual development of her children. She is a creator with unmatched tolerance and patience. Therefore, she deserves to be treated with great respect.

She is a meritorious genius and an angel in organising her family and disciplining the character of her children. She is virtuous and pious by nature, but her nature was tarnished in the course of the Middle Ages not only by men's refusal to recognise it but also by their attempt to subordinate it. Arrogant and ignorant men used their physical might to achieve their ends, and they succeeded. Women's status was downgraded, and over a long period, they developed an inferiority complex. Men took full advantage of the situation and kept women under their control.

Women were oppressed and most of their rights were suppressed. They suffered all types of atrocities and humiliation inflicted on them by men. In certain societies they were deprived of education, in others the freedom of speech. They became men's slaves.

However, the true nature of women could not be kept back for ever. The pressure women were under began to leak out when the tin container of men's domination began to erode. The container has now almost completely been eroded and its contents almost completely freed. Women can now exercise their rights and prove what they really are. Besides being a perfect parent a woman excels in her persona as a wife, a daughter, a sister, a grandparent, a scholar, a teacher, an athlete, a friend, a lover, a devotee, a spiritual leader, an administrator, a ruler and so on.

Whatever she does, she shows more love, more patience, more passion, more tolerance, more grace, more conscientiousness, more zeal, more calm and more devotion than men. The same qualities in men are somewhat weakened by their aggressiveness, their foolhardiness and their arrogance, in which they surpass women.

However, a deep-rooted weakness in women has survived till now. In spite of their greatness they are vulnerable. They have developed a liking for and a dependence on men's domination. Men are now using a new ploy to defeat women's virtuous strength, and seem to be succeeding. Instead of stopping men from indulging in such evils as drinking, smoking, gambling, defecting from spirituality and embracing materialism, hooliganism and terrorism, women are joining them. Instead of using their natural resources and creating an ideal world, which men have failed to create, women are giving in to the artificiality of mundane pleasures. Instead of propagating the glory of their spirituality, they are content with the temptation of materialism.

All is not lost yet. Around the world there are women who know their virtuous potential and are trying hard to change this topsy-turvy world into an idyllic place to live. They know they can achieve their goal if two obstacles are removed. First, they must convince the others that they are being misled by the new ploy of men and by the transient charms of materialism. Second, they must convince the power-conscious men that they must help and not hinder women's mission of changing the topsy-turvy world.

Supposing the obstacles are removed, how can women fulfil their mission? They must make full use of their innate qualities. To do so, they must be free, resolute, bold, organised and optimistic. They start their mission at home because this is where charity begins. The first role a woman plays is that of a daughter. She gives tremendous joy to the parents, who shower all their love on her and leave no stone unturned in raising her as an ideal child. Unconsciously she has already started learning the virtue of give and take.

Love and happiness are wonderful gifts to share. They are divine. They are the foundation on which Creation stands. Since love generates happiness, both are correlated. Therefore, from the dawn of her life, a woman is imbued with love. This eternal love multiplies and spreads in all directions in incredible abundance, taking various forms at different stages of her life.

This is the true nature of pure love. Since love is divine its might is next to God's. The woman expresses it in her will to make friends with all; to acquire scientific, moral, and spiritual knowledge; to establish lasting relationships with her relatives; to learn and teach good manners; to promote humanity; to preserve and improve the quality of life; and to propagate divinity. If she is steadfast, her love can never be stained by the grime of jealousy, greed, immorality, hatred, vanity, impiety, atheism and the like.

An accomplished woman, she is capable of conquering the world with love. A world conquered with love is a world of peace, freedom, prosperity and bliss. Only love can achieve such a heaven.

Alas! The vulnerability of women has weakened the purity of their love, otherwise today's world would be a heaven. But the future world can be heavenly. Therefore, it is incumbent on women to recognise their vulnerability and annihilate it. Then no power on earth can compete with them. Humanitarianism will be replaced by 'womanitarianism'.

Women must display strength in their excellence in such things as learning, upbringing, sisterhood, friendship, motherhood, morality, spirituality, caring, loving, forgiving, teaching, nursing, governing, administrating, sportsmanship, disciplining. They must demonstrate their efficiency in whatever they undertake. They do not have to prove that they deserve to be worshipped as long as they do not deviate from their true personality and divine nature.

A woman is adored throughout her life, not only for her beauty but also for the joy she radiates wherever she is, and in whatever capacity she is. When she is born everyone in the house is happy. As she grows up as an ideal child, she makes more people happy. At this stage, she relies on her first guru, her mother, who must herself be well mannered, well disciplined, educated, moralistic, spiritual, philanthropic and religious. The mother teaches her child all her own virtues and how to identify evils and stay away from them. The child learns from her father, her second guru, as well. By maintaining a healthy atmosphere in the house; by treating his wife with love and respect; by his courteous and noble manners; by his understanding; by his learned advice and puritan guidance; by his diligence; and by his justness and impartiality, he consciously or unconsciously injects idealism into the child's character. She acts and reacts in a manner that pleases all those with whom she is acquainted.

When she meets her third guru, her teacher at school, he is very pleased with her and her personality. He teaches her the philosophy of life and living and the subjects of science. She masters all the knowledge that is essential to launch on a social, educational, marital, religious or administrative career. She also masters all the qualities essential for assuring peace, freedom, national prosperity and true happiness.

The woman then becomes a lover but she does not give in to her lover's carnal desires. Instead, she explores the compatibility of their relationship. Together they try to nullify their differences. If this is not possible then their compatibility is shaky. They must not enter matrimony with a shaky relationship, but they may remain friends for ever. Usually, a woman binds the lover with a few promises. She also makes a few promises to him.

More often the promises concern bad habits, and almost always the woman has fewer of these than the man. The woman's power plays a very important role at this stage. She is possessive. She is assertive. She is influential. Her lover is attracted by her beauty, charm and warmth, which potentiate her love and mesmerise her lover.

So as not to lose her, he is willing to give up habits and hobbies like smoking, drinking, gambling, hunting, fishing, swearing, being profligate and displaying anger or conceit. The woman has already begun to mould her lover into a future responsible husband.

As a wife, her marriage vows give her more strength to continue her duty in improving the quality of life for her family and her society. As a mother, she is an inimitable, irreplaceable paragon. Her care, patience and devotion to her family, especially when a member is ill, are exemplary and monumental. She simply excels in whatever else she is: a social worker, a politician or a priestess, among others. Her responsibilities increase. Not only does she learn from her in-laws but she also teaches her children.

Her in-laws prepare her for the proper upbringing of her children and for the dutiful caring of her elders. She makes sure that her children are obedient, pious, honest, polite, caring, educated, noble, diligent, happy and healthy. She makes sure that her husband and her in-laws are well looked after and happy. She creates an idyllic atmosphere in the family. She is loved and worshipped by all because she has displayed her true nature and discharged all her duties.

The above is only a representation of a family woman, but any woman can be equally effective and revered in any field of activity where she is capable of performing. Only when a woman has ignored or undermined her strength does she fail. I have seen, heard of and read about several instances when women have dismally failed. I consider it relevant to mention a few here.

I saw a boy of ten years hitting his mother because she would not buy him a cellular phone on his birthday. The failure of the mother to teach her son from his very birth to live happily within his means was the cause.

I read about a two-year-old girl being raped by a teenager and sodomised by another. People were appalled by the hideous act. There were marches and protests against it. Marches, protests and riots do not stop these acts. The teenagers were obviously either deprived of or partially given proper upbringing. Here again their mothers were primarily to be blamed.

I heard that a woman walked out on her husband after twenty years of marriage, leaving two children in his care, all because she fell in love with someone else. I do not believe that true love leading either to wedlock or marriage vows, earnestly and solemnly taken, can be destroyed after twenty years. There was definitely something wrong in the woman's interpretation of love and marriage vows because she was not properly educated in these matters. It is of no consequence to say that the marriage did not work out, but it is imperative to find out why and seek a solution. Here again it reflects very badly on a woman's true character.

My friend was a social drinker and his wife a teetotaller for almost five years after their marriage. My friend affirmed that he would give up drinking if his wife so wished, but instead of using her influence to stop him from drinking, she joined him on their fifth wedding anniversary. Within two years both became alcoholics. Woman power was again undermined.

A beautiful woman gave up her well-paid job and became a prostitute after her friend told her that she could earn five times more by joining a call girl agency. The woman here misuses her beauty, an asset women can use to influence and inspire their men.

I can quote hundreds of instances in which the power of women has been vitiated due to improper upbringing. The sources of authority which include motherhood, schools, society and government must be incriminated in these instances. Giving women equal opportunities to men is not enough. The true strength of women, which has been suppressed for ages, must be restored first. This is not going to be easy as long as men do not accept that they have failed to create an idyllic world and as long as they do not realise that it is high time for them to give women an opportunity to try to succeed where they have failed.

While deliberating on these issues all the machineries available must be employed to restore women's intrinsic forte. Once this is restored globally, women may either create an idyllic world by themselves or most likely do it with the help of men.

I believe that women will succeed in their endeavour to create an idyllic world with the help of men and they will make no secret of it. I believe that men have failed in this mission because they did not seek the help of women, and when and where they did, they refused to acknowledge it because they did not want any part of the intended success to be attributed to women. I believe women will not make the same mistake as men. They know they need men as much as men need them. Men also have known this but they have preferred to ignore this fact. It is this knowledge that will greatly help women to succeed, because without it, or if they ignore it, they will fare no better than men.

Men can also succeed alongside women, but they must not forget that a woman is an endless source of inspiration, hence the adage: 'Behind every successful man there is a woman.' If a man forgets this power of inspiration and abuses it, the adage may well become: 'Behind every unsuccessful man there are two or more women.'

Let us for a while leave the moulding of a future idyllic world in the hands of women. When they have this duty to perform I am sure they will cast away all the bad habits men have forced on them. Then, with their praiseworthiness, rectitude, adaptability, devotion, capability, beauty, charm, love, ability to propagate bliss, power to inculcate good qualities in their children, indestructible and immortal motherhood, intelligence and love, grace, mercy, education, justice, equity, impartiality, non-violence, noble qualities, divinity, spirituality, charisma and their will and strength in perfecting any area they deal with, they will succeed in their mission. I am confident they will not fail, and our children and their children will have an idyllic world to live in.

WOMEN'S ROLE IN RELIGION

Religion must be founded on truth, logic, justice, piety and love. It must assure an important place for everybody in it. It must be universal. It must treat women as goddesses who have a special and indispensable role to play in the advancement of humanity. Sadly, by ignoring women's status, men have robbed them of their vital role for too long in this age. For too long they have been deprived of education and subjected to the humiliation and injustice of male domination in all aspects of life. They were always treated as inferior to men.

All the injustices women suffered have been slowly but not completely lifted in recent years. They were so subdued that it has taken a long time for them to recover, again not completely, from the shock of their ordeals. The wounds of their inferiority complex have not healed completely. The scars are still plainly visible, reminding them of the weaknesses forcefully ingrained in the fabric of their strength, and their place in society. Otherwise, in spite of the equality they share with men, why are they still living in a mainly male dominated world? Men are still able to take advantage of their residual weaknesses.

By leaving women in the background instead of recognising and sharing their potential capabilities, men have created a chaotic and unsafe world. Crime, killing, hooliganism, rape, drug abuse, shooting and mayhem at schools and universities, corruption, cruelties against humanity, Aids, famines, poverty, disease, environmental pollution, terrorism and all types of misery have not decreased. We express shock and horror at them, yet we are encouraging or fostering them all the time. We preach one thing and do something else. Our actions are not compatible with our wishes. For example, we preach love, but we are full of hatred; we preach philanthropy but we are selfish; we pray for peace but we create divisions in families, societies and states.

Hypocritically we organise many conferences (or are they festivals?) to resolve the global problems. The world's political, religious and spiritual leaders must stop pretending that they can solve these problems at these lavish 'festivals' unless they first come up with a system of proper education in which women participate fully, and unless they make way for women to play a major and decisive role in the running of the world. For this we must convene a global conference to discuss and adopt a globally accepted, compulsory norm of:

1. Manners and behaviour
2. Justice
3. Human rights
4. Freedom of the individual
5. Moral values
6. Education
7. Duty of the individual
8. Environment.

Because men have failed to create a peaceful world, women must be given an opportunity to reform this world. Why? Because a woman is a very important person. No creation is possible without women, and no world can run without creation. A woman is a praiseworthy human being, an empress in the family. She serves the family well and looks after everybody like a mother. She is a figure of happiness because she is humble and brings happiness to all the family members. She is a responsible person with the capacity to shoulder the burden of the whole family.

As a mother she is compared to the Earth. The Earth supplies us with all our material needs: food, clothing and shelter. A mother supplies us with our spiritual needs: love, knowledge and humanism. Both want nothing in return. Both want us to improve our lives; both want humanity to prosper. We must, therefore, hold women in high esteem, and recognise that their status in society is unrivalled.

In a patriarchal society in the Middle Ages, women's status was profaned. Deprived of her rights, the woman's role was weakened. But truth cannot be buried for ever. Women are now taking their rightful place in society. They hold the same posts as men. They are now seen in all fields of life: religion, education, politics, administration, army, space exploration and so on.

And, in spite of their professions, they have not stopped caring for their children, families, home, society, and the physical, moral, and spiritual welfare of all. However, there are three hurdles that they must overcome. First, they must shed their ingrained inferiority complex which is

1. Stopping them from confronting men's unreasonable demands on them, and,

2. Allowing men to take advantage of them.

Secondly, they must resist materialism, which is preventing them from asserting their true and inborn spiritual power. Thirdly, they must not forget that men will not easily give up their long-standing false superiority complex, and men will try all the ploys and tricks to obstruct women's endeavour to succeed where they have themselves failed. Women must realise how indispensable they are for the advancement of the human race, now that the shackles and yokes of suppression, oppression and ignorance have been removed from them. They must stand up and fight the present evils such as materialism, irreligion, superstitions and diseases like Aids, alcoholism, drug addiction, gambling, abuse of children and women, poverty, famine, terrorism, corruption, injustice, despotism and all the bad elements that have corroded and corrupted our world.

If we want the world to come out of the turmoil in which we have enmeshed it, women must offer to help. I believe that until we see what women can achieve we have no better alternative, and we must not look for one.

The Importance of Greeting

G reeting generally means welcoming someone cordially. Shaking hands brings two people together. A smile signifies friendliness. Words of greeting seal the closeness and the friendliness between people. All these can be expressed singly or collectively, to one person or to a group of people. Bowing is the humblest generally accepted form of greeting.

Embracing one another increases the depth of friendliness and closeness. Across the world there are many ways of greeting and they all have one characteristic in common – the power to dispel and banish fear and the feeling of anxiety and insecurity, and to generate friendship and the feelings of love, peace and freedom. A person can only imagine how good and exulted, free and relaxed, peaceful and contented he will feel if the people he meets, and the people who follow him, are all friends, and he has no fear whatsoever of being despised, discriminated against, jeered at, looked down upon, robbed, attacked or kidnapped, anywhere and at any time during the day or night.

Alas! In this day and age, no one can truly feel secure, free, peaceful and happy anywhere and at any time. That is why a person can only imagine the feeling and cannot really experience it. Very few people smile when you meet them, while you see angry, preoccupied, unhappy, unfriendly and apathetic people all around us, all the time. Everyone seems to be self-centred. Everyone seems to be unfulfilled. Everyone seems to be nothing other than a money-lover. He will greet you with a smile only if he has something to gain from you, especially money.

Everyone believes that money alone can solve all their problems. Everyone is running away from the problems of others while at the same time running to those they expect to solve *their* problems. Ironically, here no one wants to be self-centred and solve their own problems. It is logical to believe and preach that problems make us unhappy and unsolved problems make us unhappier. However, happiness – true and lasting happiness – is what we all want.

There are many things that contribute to happiness, but in these circumstances let us identify the root cause of happiness. We know that friendship flows towards love, love towards peace of mind and peace of mind towards freedom, and overall freedom towards happiness. But where does this friendship originate? Greeting is the obvious answer.

We start greeting one another from a very early age, even before we know what we are doing. When a baby is born and is visited by relatives and friends, the mother holds his tiny hand and waves with it, signifying that he is welcoming everyone. The baby does not know who is rich, poor, white, black, lovable, spiteful, ugly, pretty, young or old. He greets everyone alike and makes friends with everyone.

He offers his smile indiscriminately, just like a tree that offers its fruits to all alike. He can be trained and educated to uphold and promote this impartiality. It is the mother's duty to do this, but the mother must herself be impartial. If every mother raises her children in this manner no one will be an enemy or have an enemy. Friendship will prevail and with it at least one important reason for happiness. We must not forget that every sane person loves greeting babies. For this, there is one reason I can think of – the baby's love for all.

Throughout life we must keep up the importance of greeting. Often and ironically, as we grow up, we become less humble and more self-important, especially if we have achieved a higher rank in society. We shed the worthy heritage of our babyhood. We stop greeting others unless they greet us. We accuse one another of being arrogant and create an imbalance in our human relationships. Consequently, the love and friendship we should share weakens. There is a fiend waiting for this moment. It takes many forms like selfishness, disrespect and indifference. With these creeping into our lives how can we live harmoniously? Greeting one another must, therefore, be taken seriously and carried out all the time.

Sukhitapunia – Island of Contentment

My mind was very tired. It needed a rest. But rest it could not. Whenever I retired, instead of sleep, thoughts flowed endlessly in my mind, and whenever I wanted to write down my thoughts uncontrollable sleep closed my eyes for a very short while. I had reached a stage when while wondering about why it was so, I would fall asleep just for a second or two. It was as if sleep and thoughts were waging a merciless war against each other in my life.

At times it subjected me to danger and frightened me: for example, when I was driving or when I was going up and down the stairs, because my concentration could be disrupted for that short moment. I decided to stop writing, but that was a visionary decision because writing had become my obsession. I believed I had to write and warn the world of the grave it has been digging for itself. But I thought just warning was not enough. I had to think of ways to demonstrate how to save the world. That was where my problem was.

The more I thought, the sleepier I felt, and hence I could not write down my thoughts and solutions. I was extremely frustrated.

Sitting on my swivel chair, half-asleep and half-reflective, I was losing hope. Then my friend, Dino, came to pay me a visit. He looked very calm, collected, peaceful and contented. I told him about my dilemma.

'You must take a holiday in Sukhitapunia,' he advised me. 'I've just returned from there. Have you been to the island?'

'No,' I replied.

'Strange!' Dino exclaimed. 'All the ideas you've expressed in your *Beliefs and Thoughts* and those you've enlightened me with have been materialised in Sukhitapunia.'

'Is that so?' I asked, surprised.

'Very much so,' Dino replied.

'In that case, I must take a holiday there,' I said. 'Maybe I'll come up with some new theories.'

'Relaxation is what you need, my friend,' he told me. 'It's a great place for it.'

'Better still,' I said.

So I made a two-hour flight to Sukhitapunia on the island's own airline. I must say, my holiday, my relaxation, my surprises, my research, my fascination, my joy and my appraisal all started then. It was a spacious aircraft in which everyone felt as though they were travelling in first class. Cheerful, vivacious and helpful stewardesses entertained us non-stop with food, drink, smiles and sweet words. They made everyone so comfortable, relaxed and happy that it seemed tension and stress were either obsolete or had never existed. The hue of happiness did not fade a bit when we landed at Pleasance Airport, which is by the sea.

This airport is almost a see-through airport. It is a monument built almost entirely of metal and glass. Standing anywhere in it, one is able to watch the airplanes landing and taking off. With a pleasant atmosphere and a pleasing design, its attraction is enhanced by the courteous and considerate staff in any office one would care to mention. I could not help starting my inquisitive probe there and then.

It struck me that there was no secret to hide, no grilling by the immigration officers, no intimate searching or harassment by customs officers, no distinction between class, colour or creed. Every customer was treated with the same dignity, importance and warmth.

The part of the airport that quartered the toilets, shower rooms, baby-feeding rooms and that sort of thing was under-ground. I thought it would be easy to smuggle restricted items such as drugs and weapons into the country, and audaciously I asked a customs officer if there was no baggage search there. He gave me a broad smile and explained to me there was no need for a baggage search but they did carry out spot checks.

He told me that, first, the baggage had been checked by their staff at the airports of departure and secondly, they had no enemies and drug addicts, and therefore there was no need to smuggle anything in. Thirdly, their law was so strict and uncorrupted that everyone respected it. I could not believe what he told me, but I had to by the end of my fantastic holiday.

The porter who pushed my trolley to the taxi refused to accept a gratuity because he said he was paid to do his job and he was grateful for what he was earning. Before I got into the taxi I had a good look around. It was a clear day but it looked clearer because there was no pollution in the air. I could smell the scent of freshness in the mild breeze. Everyone looked healthy, fit, strong and happy and was enthusiastically engaged in some form of activity. Each person was aptly dressed for the activity he pursued.

Discipline seemed to be at its best, cleanliness at its purest. Everyone seemed to have a distinct and explicit agenda to follow. The locals greeted one another and the tourists as if they were relatives. Though Sukhitapunia is a multiracial country there was no indication whatsoever that it had more than one race in it. The taxi took me to my hotel about twenty-five kilometres from the airport.

The roads were wide and traffic was flowing smoothly, probably due to the discipline the drivers exercised and the signs they heeded. They were driving in a noticeably Apollonian manner. I was relaxed. We drove through three towns, each with its well-planned and well-designed architecture. Each open and spacious residential area was graced with tree-lined roads, large parks, playgrounds and all the necessary infrastructure.

A wider than usual avenue separated the office blocks from the industrial zone and a similar avenue separated the office blocks from the residential area on the other side. All the areas were spotlessly clean and there was the minimum pollution in the industrial area. I was told the Sukhitapunians make maximum use of solar energy. They have spent and they still spend a lot of time and resources on research into ways of producing energy without causing pollution. They believe that it is wiser to do so than to invent weapons of destruction.

They have even successfully modified their imported cars to run on solar energy. The technology they apply in most aspects of life is very advanced and they take pride in its importance alongside their spiritual, ethical, social, cultural and sporting predominance. They spare no effort in making full use of all recyclable materials.

Between the towns I saw huge gymnasiums and sporting arenas, and Sukhitapunian men and women, the elderly and the children, actively engaged in all types of sport, games and exercise. I saw huge cultural centres where men, women, and children were keenly participating in all types of spiritual, social and cultural practices. I saw churches, mosques, temples and pagodas, and prayers being conducted in them. All these buildings had wide, transparent windows, and all their doors were open. I saw schools where the teachers were conducting lessons in un-crowded classes. What I did not see was a single layabout, beggar or ruffian.

My hotel was on the east coast of the island. The welcome I received from the well-mannered, well-trained and professional staff was way beyond my expectation. I thought they were the best trained hotel staff in the world. They all showed extreme courtesy, cheerfulness, tolerance, benevolence and intelligence. But then, I realised that compared to the other Sukhitapunians I had met so far, they were really not more refined. I wondered how these people could have achieved such a high degree of excellence in their conduct and interpersonal relationships.

They gave me the impression they were not from this world, that they were from the world I had always fantasised about. I had to find someone who could give me the answers to all my inquisitive questions. I found out that I did not have to look for any specific person. Every Sukhitapunian could satisfy my curiosity. When I went for dinner I met Emme, a pretty relations officer, who invited me to her office and spent three hours answering my meticulous questions. Here is briefly what I learnt from her.

A hundred years back Sukhitapunia was an impoverished, insolvent island. The corrupt, dissolute and materialistic rulers had traded their country for a barge and fled. Sukhitapunians were starving and had given up all hope of surviving. They knew it was not altogether the fault of the rulers in flight to have caused their desperate plight. Fifty years before that there was an economic boom in Sukhitapunia, purely through the unwavering diligence and hard work of the islanders. It became a land of plenty and the islanders received whatever they asked for: massive increases in their salaries, upgrading of all infrastructures, luxuries superior to those of other rich countries, above-standard houses for all categories of citizens and plenty of time to indulge in leisurely activities.

Almost overnight, gambling institutions, nightclubs, hotels, restaurants, and amusement parks mushroomed all over the island. Consequently and simultaneously, the Sukhitapunian lifestyle changed.

When a boom is inappropriately handled it becomes a doom scenario. The Sukhitapunians did not know how to handle their island's boom. They sated themselves fully with the transient pleasures of worldliness and materialism. They squandered their wealth buying expensive clothes and jewellery, eating out in expensive restaurants, indulging in vices or just spending their money unnecessarily. They became money-lovers, but ironically they neglected or just took for granted the very thing that brought them their economic boom – hard work.

Everyone wanted easy money. Everyone wanted amusement. Everyone wanted to be free from responsibilities. Sport and leisure took precedence over work and culture; songs and dances took precedence over education and religion; eating and drinking over society and charity; and making merry over prayers and sermons. The song 'Eat, Drink and Be Merry, Brother/There's Nothing Else in Life' won the top prize in a national song contest, for even the panel of judges believed in its principles.

Gradually, most Sukhitapunians lost all sense of spirituality, morality, sociability, responsibility and other virtues. All they wanted was money, and they would get it by hook or by crook. While only a few acquired it by fair means, others used foul means. Greed befriended them. Corruption followed them like their shadows. Law and order went to the dogs. Education had only one role to play – to secure a money-making job for its pupil.

Sukhitapunia became a haven for pleasure seekers. The number of marriages decreased and the number of divorces went up. Children became naughty either because they were pampered too much or through neglect. They did not appreciate and respect the real value of money, education, society, or law and discipline. They would wreck schools and colleges and attack their teachers.

Many became mindless hooligans, many thieves and thugs and many loafers and malingerers.

Married workers with children fought for more money in their pay packets so they could give the children what they wanted and could themselves indulge in all sorts of amusements. Their rectitude and piety started to weaken and they taught very little of it to their children. Their greed for money made them selfish; their haste to outdo one another in material possessions made them irritable, impatient, intolerant, jealous, resentful, frustrated, temperamental, stressed, irate and physically and verbally abusive and violent. Diseases associated with these types of stress reached epidemic proportions.

The Sukhitapunians treated money as their god. Their belief that money and not God was their provider reshaped their attitude and mentality. They became extremely and exclusively materialistic. They bought everything with money – even their popularity, their conscience, their love, their status, their comfort, their desires, their pleasures and so on. They had no fear of God.

Vices of all types became rampant in their society. Immoral practices wrecked many marriages and homes and induced more diseases. It was as if Sodom was reborn. But they still talked money language whether it had logic in it or not.

Lost in the maze of entertainments and transient pleasures, the Sukhitapunians became a lazy, unproductive and degenerate people. It was inevitable that the boom would gradually disintegrate. To make matters worse for them, both God and gold deserted them. It is said that those who forsake God are forsaken by Him. It is also said that sloth is the root of many diseases. When the boom had completely evanesced after almost fifty years and the Sukhitapunians were harried by poverty, illness, starvation and insolvency, it was then that the rulers fled the island.

Anarchy and lawlessness emerged from the rubble of miseries. Gangs of criminals, most of whom were ironically led by marooned policemen, ruled the roost. Looting, rape, killings and other atrocities added to the agonies of the weak and the defenceless. The shops were all closed. The schools were closed. The planters ceased to grow vegetables because they were all plundered. Animal and poultry farmers, fishermen and fruiterers were all pillaged and discontinued their operations. There was more famine and more starvation.

The situation was desperate and doom-laden. People were dying by the hundred every day. The air was everywhere echoing with wails and dirges and reeking with impending plague. The islanders resumed their prayers in desperation, but they knew they would not be answered. They knew they had to pay for their sins and they were paying very dearly. They knew that if the situation lasted for another five years there would not be a soul left in Sukhitapunia.

But an unusual series of deaths revived their hope and their belief in God. A few leaders of the gangs and many gangsters were inflicted by an uncommon, deadly disease. All of them suffered horrendously for days before they died. Rumours spread like wildfire that they were the victims of the scourge of God. The remaining gangsters, dreading that they would suffer the same fate, disbanded themselves. The Sukhitapunians welcomed the little relief and peace that resulted.

Their faith in God intensified. Their repentance must have moved Him to spare them. He chose a group of intelligent and patriotic people from amongst them to pull them out of the quagmire of doom. He instilled in them the mastery of leadership and the magic to win the heart, mind and soul of every surviving Sukhitapunian. The group, self-named The Liberators, consisted of Guy, Ram, Rengen, Morris, Abdul, Dev, Lim, Noel, Ramjan and a hundred others who put their heads together and worked out a manifesto whereby they would be given the authority to govern the country.

They went round the island and convincingly presented the gist of the manifesto to the islanders, who pledged to support it, as they were made to realise they had only two options: first, to reject the manifesto and perish with those who wanted to save them; and second, to accept it, save themselves and live, totally and unconditionally, obeying its offers, conditions, demands, discipline, clauses and laws.

The Liberators were adamant that the Sukhitapunians should be completely behind them before they would initiate any negotiations with a rich country willing to bail out Sukhitapunia on the basis of the manifesto. Though the Liberators' manifesto made very stringent demands on the Sukhitapunians they preferred to approve it rather than face horrible deaths through starvation, crimes and diseases. To the drowning Sukhitapunians the manifesto was a divine raft. All of them jumped on it and held it firmly and dutifully. But what exactly was drafted in the manifesto?

Here is, as approximately as possible, how Guy presented it to the nation at one of the gatherings:

'My despairing friends, our country is sinking. We are all dying. I'm saying it's 'sinking' and we're 'dying' and not 'sunk' or 'dead'. Yes, our beloved country is sinking and we are dying, but our country is not yet sunk nor are we dead. My friends and I have a solution to avert the disaster staring us in the face. It is not a sweet solution. It is bitter, very bitter.

'Nevertheless, it is a solution, and we believe it will save us all. It is better to save our life with the bitterest of medicine than to die an agonising death. We all want to live. We all want to live happily. We, The Liberators, will give a happy life to you, to your children, your children's children and to the generations after that. We feel confident about it though we know the state, the deplorable state, of our country does not inspire confidence in what I'm saying.

'But, if we give up without a struggle, we'll be doomed, and we can't blame anybody but ourselves for it. Give us a chance to put our plans into operation. We earnestly believe they will work out well, provided we have your hundred per cent unflinching support. If you agree to give us this support, raise your hands.'

There was not a single hand that was not raised.

'Thank you, my friends. This is the type of support we're being promised all over the island. I'm glad that your will to survive by whatever means has guaranteed us your support. Now I'll put our proposals forward. But I must remind you again that the pill will be very bitter. I can guarantee you, though, that the outcome will be very sweet.

'The key to our survival is education. And we are not talking about the education that crowns us with a degree. This is also important, but this is only a part of the whole system of education, the most important part of which deals with logic, behaviour and attitude – the very essentials we neglected and consequently, brought about our own downfall. In the days when we treasured and positively exercised these essentials everyone was happy, dignified and peaceful. There was no shortage of the essential commodities of healthy and contented living.

'Everyone worked. Everyone behaved respectfully. Everyone enjoyed freedom. Wouldn't you like to return to those days?'

The crowd shouted: 'Yes, yes, yes!'

'We will give you better days than those. Right now we want your cooperation. But we must keep on reminding you that it won't be easy. We must make a lot of sacrifices in the early days. But we guarantee you, you will see better days in this life itself, and your children and their children will be proud of you for creating an idyllic place for them to live.

'Let me return to the system of education we are going to propose. We will put emphasis on and attach great importance to learning or relearning and the practice of good behaviour, manners and conduct. We must follow exemplary ethics and etiquette in our society. We firmly believe that a student who is refined in manners, polished in ethics and etiquette, and exemplary in his conduct does a great deal better than a student who is ill-mannered and undisciplined.

'Hence we're going to make the oral, written and practical examinations on behavioural, ethical, social, humanitarian and logical studies not only compulsory but also fundamental. They will be taught to everyone at all stages of his life. No student can participate in other examinations until he has passed the examination on good behaviour relating and relevant to his age and class. The students must take the following vows daily:

"Before we enter our school, we, the children of Sukhita-punia, promise to study dutifully; to revere and obey our teachers, parents and elders; to prize, cherish and guard our school; to love, respect and help one another; to have good manners and speak the truth all the time; to always use proper language; to uphold discipline and cleanliness; to refuse to give in to idleness; to be honest, just, charitable, righteous and virtuous; to be loyal to our motherland and promote her prosperity; to foster peace, freedom and humanity; to always be good and do good. May God save Sukhitapunia and strengthen our promise!'

'The teachers, the parents and the societies will be legally responsible for making the children observe the promise they will make at school. This is very important for the continuity and consistency in their observance at home, in public and at school. Unless this continuity and consistency are maintained it will be ineffective because we tend to forget or take for granted a discipline we do not exercise everywhere and all times.'

There were murmurs in the crowd and Guy heard some people saying that it would be a dictatorial exercise and commitment.

'It will seem like a dictatorial measure, but we don't think so. We think it will be a responsible measure. Everyone wants to live in a state where people behave responsibly, civilly, respectably, honestly, piously, peacefully, selflessly, altruistically and freely. No one wants to live in the state in which we are living today and stare at the face of death. We all want freedom, but freedom to live in harmony, safety and happiness. We cannot have this freedom if we also want freedom to act irresponsibly and behave asocially. Do you want freedom to behave irresponsibly and with bad manners?'

The crowd shouted: 'No, no, no!'

'Then let us make this education I'm talking about compulsory. By so doing we'll together eradicate a lot of tension and unpleasantness in life caused by violence, violation of our freedom, selfishness, animosity, injustice, corruption and other antisocial, inhumane and inhuman actions. By so doing we'll also become more tolerant, less irritable, more understanding, less apathetic, more loving, less inconsiderate, more philanthropic and less greedy. Our health will improve along with our lives.

'Now that we've all agreed on the system of education, we must work out how best we can implement it. The sooner we do it the better. But we have other issues we need to look into carefully. Work is a very important issue. We want everyone to work. Right now we must admit that we have become a nation of work-shy people. That has been the second reason for our downfall.

'We knew that we would perish if we did not take work seriously. Yet we didn't take it seriously. Why? Because our attitude and mentality changed when we were enticed by the jingle of money and intoxicated by the transient joy of an economic boom. Let's not blame ourselves for that. It was bound to happen because we had neglected our education on manners, behaviour, ethics, spirituality and humanity. We can blame ourselves for this neglect, after which money and materialism enslaved us.

'We wanted money, not work. We wanted material possessions, not education. We wanted transient pleasure, not integrity and spirituality. We had become selfish, greedy, unethical, immoral, corrupt, ill-mannered, lawless, violent and atheistic. We only cared for physical and material enjoyment. We had to pay for our sins. We paid for our sins. We're still paying for our sins. But it is time for us to repent and repair our broken-down chariot of life and move forward onto the path of righteousness, peace and happiness. We can do it if we're prepared to work hard and refrain from indulging in materialism. Are you all willing to work hard?'

The crowd shouted, 'Yes, yes, yes!'

'Very well! Let me now unveil our plan for jobs, work and occupations. Everyone will be employed. Everyone will earn a little more than what they will need for a decent and comfortable living. In that way they can save a little. If their earning lags behind for any plausible reason, the state will compensate them. Everyone will work from 0800 hours to 1700 hours daily for five days a week. Their working hours will be divided into four periods.

'From 0800 hours to noon, they will do their actual work; that is, the work for which they are recruited according to their merit. From noon to 1300 hours they will be on a lunch break. From 1300 hours to 1500 hours they will attend courses or lectures on all aspects of humanitarianism; for example, on good conduct, discipline, love, benevolence, meditation. From 1500 hours to 1700 hours they will participate in recreational and sporting activities. Two days a week this period will be dedicated to national culture and social gatherings.

'Work must be carried out with total honesty, diligence and discipline. Workers will be selected strictly according to their merits. Meritocracy will prevail in our governance and social hierarchy. Since every worker will actually be doing a half day's work, we'll need twice as many workers all the time. There will be no shortage of workers. There will be no unemployment either.

'It will be a system of sharing. Of course, the earnings will also be shared. However, we will make sure that everyone earns more than his needs will be, as I've said. We'll need many workers to monitor this system equitably and impartially.'

There were murmurs in the crowd. They had forgotten the joy of sharing.

'We know that you will find it strange to share the work and the salaries. But since you're guaranteed a decent living and no shortage of the essential commodities of life this is the best way to survive and live happily. Or do you wish to reject our plan and perish?'

The crowd shouted: 'No, no, no!'

'You're being sensible, my friends. The benefits of our proposed system of work are many. If we work hard and conscientiously and do not ask for exorbitant wages we can produce a lot more for a lot less. No other countries will be able to compete with us because this system will initially be unique. Our output will be good for the prosperity of our country.

'The second daily session of working hours is imperative. The third daily session will improve our physical and mental well-being. Consequently we'll be a happy, peaceful, united and healthy nation. Don't you all want this?'

The crowd shouted: 'Yes, yes, yes!'

'Our system will not only be envied but also copied by other countries. By then we'll have forged well ahead in the race for peace, freedom, happiness and so on. Of course, there are other issues in our system, and other systems with many issues: for example, the recruitment and formation of the police; the judiciary system; the health system; and the fiscal system, among others.

'We have to find ways to finance our systems at the outset. We've already negotiated with a rich country that is willing to finance us and offer any other help – technical, industrial and managerial – provided you all, my friends, are one hundred per cent behind our manifesto. Therefore, it is up to you to decide what you want, whether or not to go along with us, The Liberators. We'd point out very clearly to you that once you've given us your approval, there will be no backing out. We'll be indebted but we'll be in a position to pay back our debts and save our island and ourselves, because we will not commit the same mistake twice. Not only that, we'll become a prosperous and peaceful nation once again.

'Let us re-cultivate our fertile land. Let us revive the textile industries. Let us re-embellish our tropical island to attract tourists. Our warm and sandy beaches are second to none. Let us build good hotels around our island. Let us revitalise our fishing industry. Our waters are prolific in marine life. Let us introduce stock farming, new industries and new ideals.

'We'll be a nation others will envy. We'll be proud of our achievements. Everyone will be well provided with the necessary requirements of life. Our education system will ensure that we understand all aspects of life, and we do not enter any contract without fully understanding it. For example, a couple will not enter into matrimony without understanding and accepting what it means, what it requires; how and why it is a permanently binding relationship; how they must treat one another with love and affection all the time; how they must together tackle the problems of life; how they must together enjoy the sweetness of life; how they must raise their children; and how they must conduct their home life.

'Our social system will ensure that everyone is a member of a society teaching, preaching and promoting integrity, patriotism, family and national unity, good conduct and other keystones of a peaceful, happy, prosperous, healthy, law-abiding and free nation. There will be thousands of societies running along the same line. They will all be supervised by the state to ensure they do not deviate from their aims. Those who refuse to join a society will forfeit many benefits and will find it hard to cope with life. We believe there will be no one in the proper frame of mind who will refuse to join it. No one can afford to do so.

'If we are a law-abiding nation, we won't need so many police officers; we won't need so many judiciary institutions. The money we'll save as a result can be used to fund the financial and other state aids. We'll also save a lot on health because we'll be a healthy nation, as everyone will be enjoying a stress-free, pollution-free and crime-free environment. Of course, there will still be a few criminals, sick people and irresponsible citizens, as it takes time to shed old habits. However, these will decrease with time, and so will institutions dealing with them. We must shed our old habits, mentality and attitudes if we want to survive.

'There will be no personal tax. It won't be necessary. There will be no complicated forms to fill in. The state's income will come from our agricultural and industrial output, tourism and other trades, including their licences and their contributions towards pensions and so on. Since all transactions will be earnestly carried out in complete transparency there will be no wastage, extravagant spending and unnecessary projects on which millions are spent. The state will make sure that its income exceeds its expenditure.

'Thus, we'll be able to pay back our debts and start saving. The state will be relentless in this exercise. Now it's up to you to give us an unconditional mandate to incur the necessary debt to save ourselves.'

Guy interrupted his harangue for a while because he heard murmurs coming from the crowd.

'What place will there be for our religions?' one of them shouted.

Guy smiled and continued his speech.

'We, The Liberators, knew you'd be asking this question. We've not forgotten your religions, our religions. They will have their place in our society. Everyone has the right to exercise his religion in all freedom. We believe our programme will make it easier to follow our religions. Just think, my good people. Are bad people interested in religion?'

The crowd shouted: 'No, no, no!'

'Aren't we aspiring to become good people?'

The crowd shouted: 'Yes, yes, yes!'

'Are we teaching anything that contradicts our religions?'

The crowd shouted: 'No, no, no.'

'There is something, though, that we want you to understand

and accept. We don't want to mix politics with religion and vice versa, though both must not contradict each other. We hate to use the word 'politics'. We prefer to use 'good governance'. Politics, unfortunately, has given us to understand that it is a 'dirty game', because up to now, politicians have denigrated its true meaning. Misusing the power it has conferred on them, they have become corrupted, greedy, power-conscious, dictatorial, selfish, arrogant, ambitious and unpatriotic. They are elected to serve the country and its people.

'Instead, they serve their own purpose and fool their people, to achieve wealth, name, fame and power. The politicians who have fled our country after bringing miseries and disastrous consequences on us are living in luxury and comfort somewhere. They must be brought to justice. But this is not our priority. Our priorities are to find ways and means to come out of these miseries and rebuild our nation. That is why we want you to give us an unconditional mandate to incur the necessary debt urgently.'

There were murmurs in the crowd.

'I know you must all be wondering whether The Liberators will also fool you. You can't judge us until you have witnessed what we can do. We don't blame you for being sceptical but you can't deny this one chance we are giving you for the survival of all of us. I also know you're still wondering about our religions. As I pointed out earlier, we will be free to practise our religions, but we must do it at home and in our temples, churches, mosques, pagodas and other prayer places. We'll perform our rites and rituals freely, peacefully and impartially.

'The Liberators will attend them if invited but they will not use them to give expression to their political achievements in any way. We won't use religious and cultural gatherings as political platforms. The past politicians have created divisions in our society by using their influence and playing one religious group against another. We don't want to repeat the same mistake. We will move forward as one nation, one united nation, and meritocracy, not favouritism will dominate the philosophy of our government. Meritocracy is the religion of good governance.

'Good governance is not only concerned with strengthening

the nation but also with strengthening humanism. Our educational curriculum will assure the cultivation of good, loyal, upright, civil, honest, pious, peaceful, happy, educated, patriotic and humanitarian citizens. Our religions also have the same goal. So, good governance and religion follow the same path, though their ultimate destinations may be different. We believe religion takes us to the kingdom of God but we know good governance takes us to the realm of happiness, freedom and peace.

'Both destinations can only be reached when we are good and when we do good. We don't have to advertise our religion and shout in public about it to show our fidelity to God. Everyone knows that his good deeds, which include prayers at home and in other prayer places, will pave his way to the realm of God. When a person boasts about his religion, he becomes conceited, arrogant, fanatical and selfish, thus defeating the very essence of religion. When groups of people do this, they create a sense of competition, rivalry and animosity, thus defeating the very essence of good governance.

'Oddly, when religion and good governance are kept separate they create harmony and a sense of national unity. We want to create this national unity so we can all live in peace and harmony, in freedom and happiness, in security and equality. This is the religion of good governance. It is everybody's religion. That is why we want you to observe it as earnestly as you observe the religion of God.

'The religion of God alone is not enough to survive. We must also exercise the religion of good governance. We will do it. That is why we want you to give us an unconditional mandate to incur the debt to rebuild our nation. Will we get it?'

The crowd shouted: 'Yes, yes, yes!'

'The mandate is not the only demand we're making on you, my friends. We've all experienced the bitter truth about a dying, degenerate nation. We've all lost our relatives and friends. We've all seen rivers of blood and tears which are still flowing in all parts of our island. The pangs of hunger have weakened our spirit, but the flame of our resolve to survive has not been completely extinguished. It is time to proclaim 'enough is enough'. We must be earnest and honest about not only keeping the flame alive but also about stoking it with the fuel of our actions, promises to stamp out our evil beliefs and practices and the willingness to embrace all the virtuous qualities of humanity.

'We have no choice unless we want to meet horrendous deaths and leave our country for any vulturous big power to grab. Our prospective benefactor – that is, the rich and powerful country willing to help us – has assured us that it has the capacity and capability of keeping the vultures away without itself turning into one. We, The Liberators, want you to promise to cooperate fully with us before we accept the help of our benefactor. We need volunteers from all the villages and towns to fairly distribute the commodities we'll soon get. The request for food and medical help has been our priority. The help will reach us in two days.

'We must complete the formalities urgently. We have to rely on the security, fairness, honesty, and above all, the impartiality of the volunteers. We'll accept our benefactor's help in stages. The moment we detect dishonesty among the volunteers we'll dissolve our agreement. We all know what will happen if we do that. You may call it a threat or blackmail but we believe we must enforce this condition, otherwise we'll not be able to contain temptation. Do you all agree?'

The crowd shouted: 'Yes, yes, yes!'

'We've a lot to learn, and a lot to unlearn, my friends. The way ahead is not going to be easy to tread but it will not be as difficult as the path we're treading on right now. Nothing is more difficult than staring death in the face whether death is by hunger, disease or despair. However frightful, painful and horrible the agonies we're going through, let them be our incentive to fight and survive. We, The Liberators, have worked out our policies on all aspects of governance. We know how arduous they will be to implement, more so because until recently, we were used to a leisurely and indulgent life.

'We hope, though, that the hardship of the last few years has prepared us to accept the lesser hardship of the few years to come while we'll be implementing our policies, modifying them wherever and whenever necessary, and rendering them more equitable and adaptable. We mustn't expect success overnight otherwise we'll be frustrated. Frustration is one of the reasons people abandon their resolution. We don't want frustration, what we want is patience. We must have relentless patience. The impact of the implementation of our policies on all systems of governance will be fully felt and appreciated by the third generation from now.

'We mustn't forget that the folks of that generation will be none other than our children and our children's children. Very few of us will survive to see those days and they will be proud of the sacrifice and achievements of their contemporaries; that is, us – all of us.

'Therefore, for the sake of an idyllic Sukhitapunia in which our progeny will exult, let's start the mammoth task ahead of us. We must be careful, extra careful, not to give in to temptations. Temptations will try to creep into our lives because we have grown up in a world of materialism, but we must defy them, otherwise the already difficult task will become more difficult. Temptations creep in when we start forgetting how they can ruin us. We must never forget what our goal is.

'We will not, we *must* not, be afraid of difficulties. We will vanquish them. Together we will.'

The crowd shouted, 'Together we will! Together we will! Together we will!'

Guy smiled and asked the crowd if they had any questions.

'How will you cope with rioting schoolchildren?' one person from the crowd asked.

'With the education system we'll implement this question doesn't arise. The students will be responsible people who will not only recognise the negative effects of riots on education and on the welfare of the country, but will also respect their exemplary teachers and protect their indispensable institutions. We must not forget that they will acquire good behaviour, moralistic conduct and a humanitarian disposition from their parents and relatives before they start schooling. However, if ever they get out of line they will have two options to choose from: to learn and exercise discipline in freedom, or spend time in detention centres.'

'How will you deal with riots in general?' another person from the crowd asked.

'Again the question won't arise. Unhappy people riot. Everyone will be busy working for the welfare of the state, and not for its downfall. Everyone will be conscious that riots are detrimental to the state and its people. We'll do all we can to keep everyone happy. However, we can't be 100 per cent successful.

'There will be some people who will not be satisfied in life, but their number will be so minimal that the happy ones will never join them and they will naturally feel defeated and ashamed. And again, rioters, if any, will have to choose from towing the line in freedom or learning how to do it in detention centres. We cannot – no one in his senses can – afford to encourage or participate in acts harmful to the state and its people.'

A third person from the crowd asked: 'So there will be detention centres?'

'They will be necessary in the beginning because some people will not easily rid themselves of the bad habits of the past: those habits, mentalities and attitudes which have caused the present crisis on our island. When, with the full implementation of our new system of education, everyone will be concentrating on the welfare of the state and its people, riots will have no root or place in our society. There will be no place for any destructive force in our society, whether it is physical, spiritual, fictional, magical or irrational. We'll endeavour to annihilate all that is detrimental to our country, however insignificant it may appear. We'll build our nation uniquely with the materials of unity and the soul of humanity.

'We'll be the greatest united, free, peaceful and happy nation in the world. To achieve this we need your total and unflinching cooperation... devotion... diligence... honesty... impartiality... enthusiasm... and your total and unflagging effort. Are you willing to give it to us?'

The crowd shouted: 'Yes, yes, yes!'

And thenceforth the Sukhitapunians never stopped rebuilding their state and learning the endless lessons on humanitarianism and humanism. With The Liberators to persistently instil in them the formulae of survival and revival, they became obsessed with work, education, refinement of the character, renunciation of materialistic extravagance and a drastic change in their attitude and mentality. They rejected all their bad manners and replaced them with virtuous ones. They were liberally helped by their rich benefactor until they were able to stand on their own feet again. They managed that successfully in only ten years.

They clearly felt the benefit of their hard work and their ambitious education but they were not going to rest on their laurels. Now that they had tasted the nectar of true prosperity they wanted to have more of it. They aspired to become incurably and infinitely addicted to it, and passed on their addiction to their progeny. The Liberators were clever. To make sure that the Sukhitapunians did not deviate from their resolve and perseverance or relax, they kept reminding them of the hell they were living in before the start of their revival.

At the end of the decade that followed the Sukhitapunians had proudly raised a new generation of refined, rational, educated and charismatic youngsters who were patiently and passionately motivated to improve on the accomplishments of their parents and grandparents. From them new Liberators emerged who gradually replaced the outgoing ones. They did not only fervently uphold the progress achieved by their predecessors but also enriched the humanitarian qualities they inherited from them. All other Sukhitapunians religiously supported and followed them. They were virtuous people. They maintained and practised spiritual, moral, ethical and social discipline.

Vices, profligacy, dishonesty, corruption, injustice and all other disruptive activities were wiped out. The Sukhitapunians understood the true meaning of all their words, actions and conduct. They meant what they said. They took responsibility for their deeds. Their conduct was compatible with their puritan beliefs. They detested and deplored hypocrisy.

They firmly believed in lasting relationships whether they were cemented by national unity, wedlock, friendship, brotherhood, family, society, humanity or divinity, but they neither believed in nor harboured jealousy, enmity, violence, war or division and inequality of any kind (for example, family division, party division and ethnic division). Hence the family remained united and their members helped and respected one another; hence married people remained faithful to their partners; hence children did not argue or quarrel with their parents, elders and teachers; hence The Liberators worked together for the welfare of the state and its people; hence there was no division among the parliamentarians who believed they were elected to lead the nation to prosperity and not to oppose one another. They also believed the Sukhitapunians voted them in to rule and not to oppose, and there should be no opposition party. Hence societies worked in harmony. Hence there were no religious conflicts, as each individual practised his religion at home or in his religious institution. Hence brotherhood and unity prevailed.

The Sukhitapunians were no different from other people but they had made themselves different by changing their attitude and mentality when others did nothing about theirs. Obedient to their educational system, the Sukhitapunians had become ingenious, efficient and practical. They made everything simple for themselves. They knew that complicated procedures were not necessary for honest people, and that only fraudulent people necessitated complicated procedures like we have nowadays. For example, if dishonest people did not claim dole money fraudulently, the procedures for this payment would not be complicated. If people did not lie, their lives would not be complicated. Lies complicate life; honesty inspires charity.

The Sukhitapunians never had to queue unnecessarily and longer than a few minutes for anything they wanted done, for example, at the post office, hospital, bus stops and airport arrival or departure areas. Every minute was as precious as their work, which they considered to be health-promoting, life-supporting and crime-preventing occupations. They firmly believed it was a means to earn money only for the purchase of necessary things in life. Money was not given more importance than morals, nor was it greater than manners. Money was not more expedient than work.

The newborn Sukhitapunians never allowed money to corrupt them. They believed that, as money was the root of all evil, it should not control them, but it should be under their control. They were earning enough for their good, healthy, happy and peaceful way of living. Their government was earning enough through export of their manufactured goods, tourism, the fishing industry and so on to finance their education, health service, transport to and from work, adequate pensions, recreational facilities and social activities.

The Sukhitapunians had no worries, stress or frustration. They could sleep with their doors wide open. They could freely and safely roam in any part of their island at any time of day or night. They were contented with what they did possess – happiness, freedom, peace, integrity, guaranteed daily bread, safety and a prosperous future – which was a million times better than what they might like to have possessed. So, they suppressed the thought of any useless expectation. No expectation, no frustration; no frustration, no unhappiness; no unhappiness, no complaint; no complaint, no stress.

Another of the many virtues of the Sukhitapunians deserves praise and an ovation: their obsession with an unpolluted environment. No one littered the island. All of them kept it as clean as their heart. The impetus of this practice intensified with time. The Sukhitapunians never required a law to force them to maintain this because their upbringing and education were their law. They fended off many unnecessary laws, rules and regulations this way.

Nowadays, they are so efficient at keeping their environment clean that only the twice-weekly garbage collection is undertaken by the state. Shame on the other countries of the world! If litter is not cleared away and the streets are not swept for a month, they will all look like litter bins!

Human beings with true love in their hearts, unbiased and genuine nationalism in their thoughts and incorruptible benevolence in their deeds, do not require stringent laws that falsely safeguard the happiness, peace and freedom of the modern societies, which have forgotten and forsaken the innate nature of man. The Sukhitapunians had once forgotten their innate nature but as soon as they realised their mistake, albeit after learning their lesson, they never returned to that state of oblivion that was prompted by unrestricted materialism.

Since I visited Sukhitapunia, I have been entranced by the Sukhitapunians' blissful life. They get up early not to breathe the fresh air of dawn, as the air is perpetually fresh, but to pray, get engrossed in meditation and exercise introspection before they have their breakfast with their families and start their work. Half of them work from 0800 hours to noon and, after lunch, spend from 1300 to 1700 hours in educational, communal, social, cultural and recreational activities (as mentioned earlier), while the other half do the same work in reverse order. That involves the working-class Sukhitapunians, all of whom work on a monthly rotation basis.

There, work means work. No worker uses the working hours to carry out personal tasks. In my country, I must say, with a bit of shame, that many workers deal with their personal matters while customers are neglected for long periods. I am not sure that mine is the only country where this practice takes place. In my country, commoners are begging customers while the aristocrats are very important customers and no one cares.

The students in Sukhitapunia concentrate on their academic, cultural and social education. After 1800 hours they all participate in family programmes, which include preparation of food for mealtimes, homework, prayers and relaxation, and further social activities. Of course, there is special provision for some categories of workers, such as nurses, the police, hotel staff, firefighters and the staff of other essential twenty-four hour services. They have a different agenda for the day but they also enjoy the benefits of educational, communal, social, cultural and recreational activities.

The Sukhitapunians carry with them all the time the saintly halo of cheerfulness, patience, tolerance, friendliness, courteousness, love, benevolence, ethics, irreproachable manners, piety and humanism. They say that though these are very costly they do not pay anything for them. They also say that qualities like anger, hatred, stress, greed and jealousy are very cheap though they may cost them a lot. Good qualities are priceless because they generate love, friendship and good human relationships, without which it is impossible to establish peace and harmony. However, in the world we have created and are living in, some good qualities of ours may produce adverse results. In our world a smile can be misconstrued and can produce a slap, as can sweet words.

The Sukhitapunians treat their guests as their gods, with respect and extraordinary hospitality. No reasonable and fair request from a guest is ignored. I never came across an angry or a rude Sukhitapunian. Not a single vulgar or offensive word I heard coming from any of them, nor an argument. They speak softly, almost musically. The music they play is soothing and delightful.

They sing to the tune of a heartbeat and enrapture the ears. They dance to seduce the limbs. But they never allow their singing and dancing to override their humanitarian duties. Their world of music is designed to enhance the peace of mind and the exultation of the soul, and not to spawn mindless, riotous, drug-addicted, lazy and merrymaking fans.

The Sukhitapunians live in harmony and sleep in peace. Unhurried, but efficiently they perform their duties and enjoy the sweetness of a stress-free and relaxed life. They have but friends all over the world; so they have no fear. Materially, they have enough, but spiritually, they are very, very rich. They alone understand the meaning of true happiness, peace and freedom.

On my return from Sukhitapunia, I asked myself one question: must every nation in the world undergo the plight of the materialistic Sukhitapunians with their booming economy before the negativistic and destructive attitude and mentality of its people changes?

Having awakened the materialistic world of today from its complacence with the story of Sukhitapunia, I have one fear – one big fear: I will be ignored or called a dreamer. My misfortune!

But... why are we living in a world in which thousands of crimes are taking place every second? Why are we praying for peace everywhere and every day of our lives while we do very little or nothing to avert suffering? Why are we building a palace for technology while we are unable to build a hut in which to house humanity? Why are we seeking lasting happiness while we are sated with the transient pleasures of modern-day life? Why are we living in a world full of hatred, jealousy, greed, injustice and violence, and day by day amplifying them?

Why are we living in a world rife with poverty, famine, disease, war and terrorism? Why are we reshuffling the cards of our education if we have no intention of improving it? Why are we summoning so many conferences if we are not improving the quality of our attitude and mentality? Why are we harbouring superficial or artificial instincts while destroying the natural and virtuous ones?

The answer to all these questions is simple. We are hypocrites. We know what is wrong yet we do it. We know what is right yet we do not do it. For example, we know we must not eat unhealthy fast foods yet we eat them. We know we must be humble yet we are arrogant.

The world leaders know that the right education teaches us the right attitude and the right mentality but they prefer to keep and cherish the system of education that is responsible for wrong attitudes and mentality. We all know that clean air is more important than money but we run after money only and care for our health only when it is affected or when we are frightened of the afflictions its impairment may cause us. There are thousands of examples that demonstrate our hypocrisy.

In Sukhitapunia nowadays, people do not have the wrong attitude and mentality. The citizens do not damage government property such as buildings and police cars. They are sensible. They know that the property is their own as they themselves are the government. They know that damaged property has to be replaced and that costs money, which they know must be wisely spent and justly used. The students do not damage their colleges because they know that it is sacrilegious to destroy the very place where they acquire an education, which is sacred to them. They believe it is like fouling the very plate on which their food is served.

They do not attack or kill one another because they genuinely want to live in peace, and they genuinely believe that attacks and murders are inhuman and are the acts of sick people. Instead of promoting peace, these actions destroy it. The Sukhitaputians also believe that anger, hatred, vendettas, impatience, violence (physical or verbal), threats and the like do not solve any problems. They increase them. They consider day-to-day normal problems as an integral part of life and they can be solved easily with wisdom, love, calmness, understanding, friendliness, civility and the right mentality and attitude.

They believe that human beings are themselves responsible for creating problems, and they are also capable of dealing with them without allowing them to cause stress, tension, anger, despair and other emotions.

The Sukhitapunians are unhurried, patient, careful, efficient, agile and confident people, and are, therefore, unlikely to provoke accidents, though accidents, they say, cannot be completely stamped out anywhere in the world. They are law-abiding, educated, peaceful, loving, friendly, considerate, God-fearing and selfless; and are, therefore, unlikely to commit crimes and offences. Police, ambulance or firefighters' sirens are rarely heard in Sukhitapunia, adding to the tranquillity one enjoys there.

The Sukhitapunians do not use swear words or offensive language. They know that these are terms used by uneducated and/or angry people, and they are verbal or written missiles that hurt those they are hurled at. No one needs to have recourse to these terms if he speaks his language well. No one needs to offend others, but everyone needs to respect and protect others if we want this world to enjoy good humanitarian relationships, as in Sukhitapunia.

The standard of living in Sukhitapunia may not be as high as that in many other countries, but the quality of life is beyond comparison. On that island everyone is happy – truly happy – peaceful – truly peaceful – and free – truly free – because there is no homelessness, unemployment, poverty, famine, hatred, violence, hooliganism, injustice, corruption, pollution, discrimination, tension, man-induced disease or fear. Everyone has what he needs. They do not crave extravagant luxuries. They do not embrace promiscuity, alcoholism, drug addiction, gambling and unproductive entertainments. They do not suffer from illnesses like Aids, depression, obesity and leprosy. They enjoy good health, take healthy food and live longer. They have made all this possible by their well-planned work, educational, social and recreational programmes, and by their good governance. They are very advanced in technology but even more in humanism and humanitarianism.

There is a clear-cut and phenomenal contrast between Sukhitapunia and the rest of the world. While the rest is witnessing increasing negativistic and detrimental events in life, such as disease, crime, accidents, murder, terrorism, corruption, injustice, violence, poverty and famine, Sukhitapunia is enjoying an increase in the positive and constructive aspects of life such as impeccable human relationships, good governance, clean environment, integrity and freedom.

For the survival of humanity globally, it is better to rely more on spiritual prosperity and less on materialistic property. Technical advancement combined with moral deterioration may bring disaster, but moral advancement combined with technical success will definitely avert disasters. For example, if something goes terribly wrong with computer technology because of some mindless disseminator of bugs, disaster will be inevitable. We must not forget that any little matter nowadays, even if it is minutely offensive, can threaten the fragile peace of the whole world.

Governance

To manage a household, an organisation or a state, the most important elements are resources in all their capacities and contexts. The aim of management is to accomplish a permanent and progressive happy atmosphere. When the resources are available the task is easy, provided they are used with efficiency, proficiency and impartiality. Any deviation from these, however minute, spells failure and collapse. The most substantial and considerable resource is manpower. No household, organisation or state can possibly exist without adequate manpower. None does, except where governance or management also does not exist.

A household, an organisation and a state are all born. In other words, they have a beginning. I believe whatever is born must one day die. Whatever has a beginning must also have an end. Men are responsible for the births of households and organisations. It is, therefore, incumbent on men to take on the responsibility of caring for them, just like a man's responsibility to care for his children.

The type of care decides the lifespan of a household, an organisation or a state. Good, consistent and wholehearted care prolongs life. Neglect shortens it. No individual wants to shorten his life, though he knows his life will end one day. If he is unhealthy he tries to get well. If he is poor he tries to get out of poverty. If he is uneducated he tries to seek education. If he is well, he tries to be better. He tries to dispel ignorance and misery and improve his knowledge and happiness. Man is born with these instincts. He is also born with the instincts to refine his household and his state, but nowadays these instincts are overshadowed by selfishness. That is why man does most for himself and less for his household and his society, and least of all for his state. This is the root of disintegration.

Inquiry

What do men need to do?

Statement

Obviously we have to remove the cause.

Inquiry

How?

Statement

Let us identify every aspect of manpower in minute detail and see how to achieve its maximum potential, eliminating all its negative qualities, otherwise it loses its importance. We all know that a human being is the highest form of life. He is endowed with both constructive and destructive powers, which are tremendous. When man releases his constructive powers, which he is intelligent enough to recognise, he is substantiating his greatness, and his superiority over other species. But if he releases his destructive force, which he is also intelligent enough to recognise, he is showing his lowliness and proving his inferiority to other species. What makes man superior to theirs is obviously his intelligence.

I believe intelligence must be used only to achieve a worthy goal. The most worthy goal of man is to create a peaceful world for everyone to share. It naturally and obviously follows that such a world cannot exist as long as wars, famines, poverty, diseases, slavery, riots, terrorism and unhappiness caused by injustice, corruption, misgovernment and other things rampage all over its surface.

In this context it can be argued that other species are superior to human beings in this day and age. For example, a bird uses its intelligence to achieve only what nature has intended it to do. It knows where, when and how to build its nest; when and where to migrate; what to feed on; and how to communicate with its own kind. It does exactly that and lives in peace. So does a dolphin or a chimpanzee. They do not endanger themselves or others of their own kind. It is true that they also fight, but it is not known that birds, dolphins or chimpanzees have fought among themselves so as to annihilate their own species.

If they did they could be excused because they are inferior forms of life. But how can men be excused when they kill themselves by the millions whether with wars, diseases, for which they are themselves responsible, or through famines they can avoid? Famines caused by droughts, floods and poverty can be averted if men do not misuse their intelligence and ignore good governance. During good times men forget the hardship that may lie ahead.

My mother used to tell me a story. There was a monkey who was shivering with cold at night when winter approached because he did not have a proper shelter. He promised himself that the first thing he would do the following day was to build a shelter. When the day came he saw fruit in abundance all around him. He enjoyed eating it all day and forgot about the cold weather that followed at night. He shivered again and he promised himself again that he would build himself a shelter the following day.

He enjoyed the fruit again the next day and forgot about the cold night. The scenario went on for days until he contracted pneumonia and died.

This story reminds me of countries prone to floods and droughts where the corrupt and greedy politicians and their supporters have a good time with the money their countries yield instead of using it to strengthen their countries and meet their requirements. When the money is spent, they go around begging for loans to have more good times. They do not care about their country's shelter or the pneumonia lurking ahead. They neither use their intelligence constructively nor their power objectively. This is sheer bad governance.

Manpower, like man himself, has two qualities: one which is tangible or physical and the other which is intangible or spiritual, just like the body and the soul. One cannot exist or function without the other, though one can overshadow the other. To achieve the best results in the governance of a state, the spiritual and the physical aspects of manpower must work with cooperation and be in harmony, but they cannot work together if they are not properly trained. Training must start before the household or the state is set up. Here it must be borne in mind that running a state is not as easy as running a household and that the training for running a state is more stringent and methodical.

The training for the governance of a household is carried out mainly through observation, experience, maturity and circumstantial necessity. It can be called a growing-up process.

Good governance involves every citizen, whether in the public sector or in the private sector; whether he is a schoolchild or an adult; whether he is married or single; whether he is rich or poor. Every citizen must be well educated and noble. He must be diligent, righteous and virtuous. Every person is important because he is responsible for the role he plays. For example, a police officer must be courteous, helpful, just, sympathetic and understanding. A nurse must never forget that the patients require a lot of patience. A good trader cannot afford to be angry with his customers. A schoolchild must show respect to his teachers, parents, society and school, not forgetting that he may be one of the future politicians. Politicians must work only for the welfare of the country and its people. Everyone must be worthy of the job they do. If every citizen takes their responsibilities seriously, good governance can be achieved. Unfortunately, these days there are too many misfits and corrupted people in any government one cares to mention, and the good governance we talk about does not really exist. There is no Sukhitapunia around.

It is sad that every government in the world has an opposition, legitimately or illegitimately. It is sad because though opposition does not mean acting in any way that is detrimental to the country and its people, it is doing exactly that. Those who oppose a government must always come up with ideas that are constructive or more constructive than those of the government. The government must also always act for the welfare and prosperity of the state. If the opposition acts in a manner that is harmful to the state there will always be chaos because there will always be a government and an opposition. If both act for the advancement of the state, peace will prevail.

Consequently, if this philosophy is applied globally, the whole world will be at peace. There are learned people on both sides. As a matter of fact, only learned people must be parliamentarians, because it is never the way of learned people to destroy their own countries. Acts such as riots, strikes, bombings, killings, terrorism and causes of divisions in a nation are destructive forces. They must never be contemplated or carried out. It is the duty of the government and the opposition to prevent such acts. If human beings, especially learned ones, cannot understand this they are themselves to blame for the downfall of their countries and they are not worthy of being human beings.

Only animals fight physically and violently to protect their territories. Human beings are no different if they do not use their mental and intellectual strength and superiority to resolve any problem. As a matter of fact, when all human beings are properly educated and become noble, problems will not arise at all, because negative qualities such as greed, jealousy, covetousness, power consciousness, possessiveness, selfishness, hatred and the like will not exist. Everyone will be loving, caring, generous, humble, selfless, just, pacific, gentle, understanding, moralistic and pious.

The peace we are so frantically and earnestly seeking will be present in each individual's life; in each society; in each country. The government and the opposition will become one and they will work for the prosperity of all, because only those capable of holding the reins of good governance will be entrusted with this duty. Besides, are not all politicians voted in to govern and not to oppose?

I remember the serenity that reigned in my village when I was ten years old. Though only a few people were educated, everyone lived in peace and communal harmony, helping each other all the time. There were no walls between properties. Access to all parts of the village was free. The doors had no locks and were left open because the villagers were all good people and there was no fear of burglary, rape and killings. If the doors were closed it was for a bit of privacy or to prevent cats and dogs from entering the houses or to shelter ourselves from inclement weather.

The elderly, the old and the sick were well looked after and respected. Families were close-knit. The villagers knew and protected one another. Everyone worked and lived happily. Now, if such a condition could prevail in a village where mostly uneducated people lived, I cannot see why it cannot prevail in villages, towns and countries where learned and educated people live. All we have to do is to rid ourselves of the negative qualities which have gradually crept into our lives and are destroying our modern world.

How did these negative qualities enter our lives? One answer lies in bad governance. Governments did not ensure a continuous build-up of good qualities that once prevailed. Instead they allowed money and materialism to overshadow our virtuous qualities; they allowed amusement and recreation to overshadow our culture and education; they allowed all forms of transient pleasures to overshadow our sense of duty. There is no bigger temptation than money. Money has captivated the whole world.

No one does anything without money. The word 'voluntary' has become outdated. Everyone is running after money, no one more so than the politicians. Money has corrupted everyone. The more we have, the more we want. It has buried our virtues and dug up our vices.

And we all know that corruption is the greatest cause and evil of bad governance. And we all know that there is no government in the world that can claim total immunity from corruption. Corruption is likely to increase globally because we are becoming more and more materialistic and less and less spiritual. It requires a brave government to reverse this trend.

We have made gigantic progress in technology, which has become the obsession of all governments. It has become necessary in this day and age, but the decadence of humanity is also spreading fast. One has only to study the behaviour of schoolchildren, sports fans, religious fanatics, drug and alcohol addicts, the carriers and victims of Aids and other diseases, the world of prostitution, the instigators of crimes, promiscuous society, hooligans, divorce seekers, corrupt politicians and high officials, insolent public and the pleasure seekers to see what I mean.

One does not even have to carry out a profound study to realise that governments are not doing enough to arrest this decadence, let alone try to decrease it. Is this the sign of good governance? Is it not the duty of a good government to fight decadence so as to uphold the progress of technology? It is said that if finance is left in the hands of a good and honest treasurer, the treasury will for ever be full.

If we end decadence we shall be left with good people: good people form good governments; good governments produce good governance; good governance pleases people. We can, therefore, deduce that good people make themselves happy, and therefore, we must all be good. To be so, we must educate ourselves and discard all our bad qualities. Are we ready to do that? The answer is yes, because we all want to be happy, free and peaceful.

Good governance is achieved by:

1. The wise use of manpower.

2. The implementation of proper education.

3. The unprejudiced enforcement of law and order.

4. The transparent and economical handling of finance.

5. The prosperity of trade and commerce.

6. The protection of people's welfare.

7. The preservation of a healthy environment.

8. The establishment of lasting peace and happiness.

9. The motivation, supervision, and assistance of societies dealing with religion, culture and national welfare.

10. The avoidance of poverty, unemployment, and shortage of essential commodities.

11. The creation of sporting and recreational establishments.

12. The prevention of riots, acts of terrorism, strikes, crime and decadence.

13. The establishment of good relations with the rest of the world.

14. The exploitation of all productive resources.

15. The encouragement and support of national unity and harmony.

16. The eradication of corruption, divisions and inequalities.

17. The minimisation of accidents in all fields of life.

18. The continuous improvement of good governance.

19. The assurance of a constant betterment in the quality of life and the standard of living.

20. The ability and efficacy to tackle national disasters.

21. The provision and safeguard of adequate educational institutions.

22. The creation of a guaranteed future for the nation.

23. The development of adequate hospital and auxiliary services.

24. A sound infrastructure for the electricity supply, water distribution, sewage disposal, roads, and public transportation.

25. The provision of houses to the needy.

26. The observance of meritocracy.

Educated human beings are quite capable of implementing good governance. There is nothing we cannot achieve if we do not deviate from the humanity that is in all of us. All we need is willpower and perseverance. We must all be prepared to act for our own good. We must act.

Education

Education is the key to success in attaining global peace, prosperity and freedom. It covers a vast area. We have made tremendous progress in many fields, except in those that *matter most*: namely ethics, etiquette, human relationships, communal and multiracial harmony, philanthropy, neighbourliness, altruism, philosophy, love-sharing, spirituality and above all, discipline. Unless these are studied first and everyone achieves a degree in each of them, all other studies cannot guarantee individual, national and international peace, prosperity and freedom. A hundred-storey building will sooner or later crumble if the fifty top storeys are sound and well-equipped while the lower fifty storeys are unsafe and poorly equipped.

We cannot reach for the sky standing on a wobbly foundation. This is exactly what we are doing. We are trying to reach the zenith of perfection in technology without fortifying the platform of the studies that *matter most* for the survival of the human race. How long can we survive?

Fortunately, many of us have realised our plight and want to do something to save humanity. Unfortunately, realisation and desires are not enough. We need action – quick, calculated and positive action. Our greatest stumbling block is our egoism. Everyone is too busy amassing material possessions. They have no time to do anything for others. They are not aware that if they want to realise their desires, they have to shed their egoism first. For this they must take a refresher or a beginner's course in the studies that *matter most*. It means that we must all go to school and acquire a proper education – an education that includes all the subjects and especially that gives priority to the subjects that *matter most*. This is what we must do for ourselves. What we must do for the future generations is to ensure that they will not have to take a refresher course.

We will teach them from their very early days. We must,

therefore, start building the foundation of their education straightaway. Therefore, straightaway we must start *our* refresher course, which is very important because we have either forgotten or prefer to ignore a lot of knowledge passed on to us from our fathers and forefathers. For example, we know we must be polite, yet we are rude; we know we must love one another, yet we hate one another or pretend to love one another; we know we must not be greedy, yet we want more than our needs.

We know that we must be logical, yet we support illogical beliefs and practices. We know we must do most for our country, yet we want our country to do most for us. And so on and so forth. This sort of mentality is not limited to some countries only. It is worldwide. I was walking along a promenade in England where it was clearly signposted in many places 'No Cycling', yet cyclists were ignoring the notice. I saw pedestrians crossing roads in Singapore where it was forbidden to cross. I saw motorists driving over the legal speed limit in America. These people audaciously swear at passers-by who try to remind them of the regulations. Why do we do it?

In my opinion, the answer to the above is simple. We are living in a world of materialism, which we have ourselves created and in which little importance, if any, is attached to spiritual, ethical and social values. It is designed to wreck the peace, freedom and ideology of human relationships, which we are all foolishly seeking; foolishly, because we are zealously harbouring and exercising our materialistic mentality. Our preference is wrong.

The day we seriously, willingly and religiously allow our spiritual, ethical and social interest to override our materialistic interest we will not need any law to tell us how to behave and conduct ourselves. Genuine humanism will reinstate itself globally. Peace will prevail. We will all experience a true sense of freedom and lasting happiness. We will all live harmoniously like a colossal united family. But how do we achieve this idyllic state?

The answer lies in proper education. An individual's education starts well before he is even born as I have mentioned before – at the time when his ideal parents start courting one another with a view to enter matrimony. It is the preparatory stage. They discuss when they must marry, when they must start a family, how they must conduct themselves when the wife is pregnant, how the child will be educated and how they must raise him. After discussing the complete preparation of the individual's education and upbringing and reaching a mutual agreement on all aspects of their conjugal life, they take the necessary step – marriage.

They must not deviate from the education they have themselves been through – the education that has made them ideal individuals. I explain this in my book *Beliefs and Thoughts*.

Due to a lack of proper education, the number of criminals, hooligans, terrorists, debauched and despotic politicians, corrupted officers and bad people is increasing. Every day we learn with horror the different atrocities and hideous crimes committed by these monstrous people. The crimes include rape horrendously carried out, mass murder and genocide among others of less atrocity. We do not try to either understand or realise that:

1. These monsters are the products of the society we have ourselves created.

2. We are continuously creating more monsters.

3. There are many more crimes to come.

If we want a clean and salubrious environment it is no good creating and cleaning pollution continuously. We must stop creating pollution. Similarly, we cannot get rid of hooligans, terrorists, despots and similar people if we go on creating more of them, and the only way to stop creating these monsters is by the right education from the right moment. We must have global conferences to tackle this issue. I believe the feasibility of compulsory induction of global manners and conduct, behaviour and morals, and other human values into the curriculum of education at all stages of life, from birth to death, must be seriously considered.

I believe this is the only way to annihilate the monsters. All the countries of the world must become Members of Global Educational System (MOGES) and conform to the code of global ways of life aimed at creating and promoting global peace, justice and liberty. People in countries not willing to join MOGES will not enjoy the privileges of the people of MOGES countries, should they wish to visit or trade with them.

I have already made some suggestions on education and other issues to be tackled by international conferences under other headings, and repeating them is not my intention. But I must reiterate that it is imperative to ameliorate our education system.

The Religion of Man

I have expressed my views on the causes of mayhem gnawing at our peace, happiness, liberty, prosperity and welfare. I have attempted to tackle the main issues behind this mayhem: education, the role of women, governance, pollution, humanism, human relationships and discipline, among others. The religion of man has prompted me to do so, because the religions men are following nowadays have derailed them from the track. The Religion of Man is truth. It teaches us to be good and do good.

We must be loving, caring, friendly, just, impartial, benevolent, moralistic and humane, and above all, united. The religions we are following are dividing mankind, and what is worse, we are not only refusing to accept this but we are also continuously adding fuel to it, by anger, greed, violence and other destructive qualities, thus increasing suffering throughout the world, even in the quasi-peaceful countries.

I believe the Religion of Man is in vast contrast to the religions men follow nowadays. Religions have become very fragile and the followers are easily provoked. The adherents have become too sensitive and fanatical and ready to disrupt any peace that the world is enjoying. The Religion of Man, on the other hand, is divine and cannot be provoked however hard we try. Those who follow this religion are unperturbed by any mud thrown at it because they know that it can never be sullied by any amount of mud. It is like gold that does not fade with time or grime. It is like the sun that never withdraws its warmth from those who spit at it, because it knows that the spittle always drops on them.

The Religion of Man is the right religion. Religions that are responsible for spreading hatred among people and causing millions of deaths cannot be right. Right religion has no other aim than the advancement of humankind. There are too many wrong religions uncontrollably spreading over the surface of this world, and I prefer not to dwell on them any more than I deem necessary.

Besides, I have no intention of confusing the already confused irreligious people, which I believe we have all become, otherwise why do we differ and quarrel in the name of religion? I do not believe that God created so many religions without consistency within them – they even contradict each other. Rites and rituals have become showpieces. Many religions are sanctioning them. They cannot be the right religions because they are creating divisions in mankind. Ironically, many volumes have been written about them, and very few about the Religion of Man.

The laity can easily understand this. Unfortunately it is the laity who believe more positively that the religions they follow are the right ones. It is not their fault. They have been brainwashed for too long into following traditions and traditional rites and rituals. They cannot break away from their culture so easily, so quickly. This is made more difficult for them by the continuous and rapid changes in our culture today. Also because religions are competing against each other, some old practices are being revived, adding to the confusion of the laity.

The grown-up children who like to believe in logic and truth, are rebelling against the beliefs of their parents. This rebellion has driven them into the world of materialism. Money, and not morality, means everything to them. Talks by eminent scholars and pundits do not have an impact on them because these talks involve God and gods. That is why it is necessary to talk to them in simple terms and inculcate in them the logic of why it is necessary to be good and to do good without frightening them with what God has in store for them if they are not good. They do not fear God but they will see reason in the philosophy of humanitarianism in which He manifests Himself.

There is, however, one aspect of life that most youngsters do not want to give up. They want to have religious weddings in churches, temples, halls or in the open – and they want their weddings to be grand. They also want some other rites and rituals performed according to the religions we follow. It means they are not totally materialistic. They still realise there is a God and have faith in Him.

As long as the Religion of Man – humanitarianism – is not forgotten or ignored we shall have hope for global peace, freedom and justice, because this religion unites the world and its population. It has no weapons to create divisions because it is consistent throughout the world. Let us adopt it. We must also adopt the goodness of other religions whatever its proportion in them; but we must reject all that is bad, false, illogical, superstitious and unnatural. Let us see God through the Religion of Man and not through those we are blindly following, because the laity cannot grasp the meaning of God as easily as the scholars, seers and saints.

It is easier for us to see the miracles of God in and through objects and people He has created than through unexplained phenomena or incredible myths, but because we have been misled I believe 98 per cent of us directly or indirectly believe in and pray in front of icons; otherwise, since God is omnipresent, we do not have to face any direction when we are praying.

In the Religion of Man, we do not fully comprehend God, but we pray to Him to protect the welfare of all beings; to help us establish global peace and prosperity; to lead us to our freedom and justice; to give us good health and happiness; and to help us build a better future for our children. But our own willpower, perseverance, hard work, integrity and humanitarianism are required for our prayers to be answered.

I also believe that the Religion of Man and the religions we follow have many attributes in common. Both stipulate that God is merciful, just, omniscient, omnipresent, omnipotent, all-energy, without beginning or end, and Creator of all that exists. Both require men and women to be humble, forgiving, impartial, friendly and united. What they teach us to be and what we are, differ tremendously. We have only to think deeply and sincerely and ask ourselves: are we really humble or arrogant?

Are we really friendly towards the rest of the world or are we aggressive towards it? Are we really impartial or are we prejudiced? Are we really forgiving or vindictive? Are we really united or (perhaps) irrevocably divided? How many of us can honestly boast of having banished jealousy, greed, conceit and so on from our hearts? Let us seek, each one of us on our own, the answers to these questions.

I discern around me the animosity between brothers and

brothers, sons and fathers, brothers and sisters, neighbours and neighbours, countries and countries, religions and religions, and even in many cases, between husbands and wives. How can we, therefore, claim to be united? There is also, quite ridiculously, a lot of animosity between people of the same religion. They are killing each other by the thousands while pretending to be united. We are really confused. We do not know what we really want.

It is sad to see that, after bitter struggle, a nation achieves freedom and independence only to watch its own people killing each other and destroying the fruit of that bitter struggle. This sort of situation is not confined to just one nation. It is very widespread.

We are no more abiding by the attributes that are common in the Religion of Man and the religions we follow. Instead, we are harbouring and cherishing the common attributes of irreligion. This is where we have gone wrong. This is what we must put right. It is never too late to mend; and nothing is impossible if men work together. Let us follow the good attributes of both the Religion of Man and those we have adopted and build a world we shall exult in.

Routine or Duty?

An individual must not perform his prayers, pujas and other religious observances as a routine but as a duty and a necessity. In this day and age, they must also be performed as an urgency. Our life is polluted to the core with the evils of materialism. We must purge ourselves of these evils, which include anger, greed, hatred, jealousy, animosity, conceit, prejudice and selfishness among others. Spirituality alone can cleanse us.

We clean our house daily and we believe we are doing it as a routine. This is not true. Dust settles every time in every nook and corner of our house. It is necessary to clean it daily. If we do not the germs in the dust will multiply and diseases are likely to develop and spread. Dusting and cleaning is, therefore, an urgency. Similarly, we wash our clothes when they are dirty; we clean our environment when it is polluted; we have a bath when we are unclean.

We would not have to lock our doors and windows and activate our alarm systems if there were no burglars. Carrying out this exercise has become a necessity. We do not open our windows in the morning as a routine but to allow fresh air to circulate, because it is necessary for our health. We do things out of necessity and it seems like a routine. There are things we do which are not necessary yet we carry them out routinely; for example, some people go to pubs every day, others go to gambling houses daily and some go to the races frequently and regularly. For convenience, we perform certain necessary acts regularly and systematically; for instance, some people do their weekly shopping on Saturdays and others on Fridays or Sundays.

Whatever we do must carry the hallmark of four plausible and positive reasons; namely, necessity, urgency, benevolence and spirituality; otherwise our actions are futile. Let us analyse the reasons for the four vital actions in our lives: prayers, food intake, work and social activities. In my book *Beliefs and Thoughts* I have outlined the importance of these. However, there are other points which I believe are worth mentioning.

Prayers are important because they purify our souls and inspire us not only to perform noble acts but also to avoid and refrain from practising evil ones.

Inquiry

How and why?

Statement

The goal of the soul is to achieve salvation; call it paradise if you wish. We know that noble deeds alone can help the soul achieve its goal. What does someone who prays ask for in his prayers? In one word – happiness, which, of course, covers a range of other factors. He cannot be happy if he has no peace, freedom, prosperity, wealth, good health, loving family and neighbours, good friends, a caring society or an idyllic country.

Surrounded by warring, feuding and aggressive people, he cannot be happy. Surrounded by slaves he cannot be happy. Surrounded by poverty and diseases he cannot be happy. Surrounded by unfriendly families, neighbours and society he cannot be happy. Living in a badly governed and chaotic country he cannot be happy. Surrounded by violence and vices he cannot be happy. Surrounded by pollution he cannot be happy. Surrounded by evils he cannot be happy. If he prays for happiness and his prayer is granted he gets a lot more than he asks for, because happiness comes with many other benefits. And unconsciously he is praying for everyone's happiness, peace, prosperity, good health, freedom, wealth and goodness, because he can only be really happy when everyone else is really happy.

If he is praying for everyone's happiness it is not possible for him to think ill of anyone, to bring misery on anyone, or to make an enemy of anyone. If he prays earnestly and sincerely his actions can only be noble and praiseworthy. Such actions alone are necessary nowadays for global peace, freedom and happiness, and they are inspired by the power of prayers.

Inquiry

Are you saying that a person who does not pray cannot be inspired to perform noble acts?

Statement

An earnest prayer is a commitment, a binding contract to carry out an undertaking. Signing such a contract is a prayer in itself because it becomes an obligation, a duty. (No one in his proper frame of mind signs a contract to perform an evil deed.) What he does, therefore, is a noble deed because his signing is the inspiration to fulfil this deed. Signing a contract is a physical exercise whereas praying is a mental and spiritual exercise, which is more binding. While one involves his legal commitment the other involves his moral conscience.

Inquiry

Why does a person have to be considerate and perform deeds for the welfare of others?

Statement

In the welfare of others is his own welfare. No one wants to be hurt. It is, therefore, incumbent on a person not to hurt others. Similarly, no one wants his welfare to be hampered, and therefore, it is incumbent on him to work for the welfare of others. If he is not considerate he is likely to hurt others. That is why everyone must be considerate.

In this way we come to respect and love one another. Respect and love promote friendship. Friendship promotes peace. We all want peace in the world. Peace is one very important ingredient for the recipe for happiness. Happiness is what we pray for.

If we want our prayers to be answered we cannot just sit and pray. We must also perform deeds which promote the welfare of all. If we just pray without noble actions our prayers are useless, no matter how many times a day, or how loud, we pray. Noble actions result from noble words and noble thoughts. Prayers inspire us to think nobly, as I have proved in my earlier statements. We must not forget that noble actions are also a form of prayer, or rather a continuation of prayers.

Inquiry

What is necessary to achieve salvation or enter paradise?

Statement

Worldly happiness resulting from the prayers, noble deeds and love exercised by everyone is heaven; suffering is hell. True and everlasting happiness is our ultimate goal; that is, salvation. To achieve this the soul must be pure. The soul attains purity through deeds inspired by earnest prayers. That is why I maintain that prayers purify the soul and they are performed as a duty, not as a routine.

Inquiry

Food intake is a necessity and an urgency. How do you associate it with benevolence and spirituality?

Statement

Simple. Meals must be of good quality, in adequate quantity and complete; that is, it must not be stale, unhealthy, heavy or deficient in anything that the body requires, such as fat, carbohydrates, protein, vitamins or minerals. Of course, the requirements can vary from body to body, and also depend on the activities, sex, constitution and metabolism of the person. Proper meals must be taken at proper times and consistently. I do not believe fasting is important if these conditions are respected. If they are fulfilled, fasting for any reason and any amount of time can be harmful to the body, for it produces imbalance in the digestion and renal functions, flatulence, constipation and other physical and mental discomforts. If we try to run a car without water, oil or air pressure we will cause it a lot of damage, and we cannot drive it without fuel. In the same way we cannot live without food and we can damage our body by depriving it of its needs. Hence I believe fasting is harmful. If we believe God has given us this perfect body and shown us the right ways to keep it healthy, He could not have decreed fasting, otherwise He would be contradicting Himself. There is no doubt that fasting causes discomfort but we accept this discomfort.

Inquiry

People train their mental state to control or neutralise these discomforts before they fast. It is a question of mind over matter.

Statement

I still cannot find a valid and plausible reason for fasting. If we want to train our mental state, we must train it to control our food intake because we all indulge in unhealthy fast foods or overeat when the food is proper and good. Controlling our food and food intake is an important exercise for the mind, and this is very important for our health. Because we cannot keep up with this exercise, we are always eating the wrong food, in the wrong amount and at the wrong times. I still maintain the intake of regular, complete and adequate meals is best for our physical and mental health.

When we are healthy physically and mentally we can totally concentrate on benevolence and spirituality, otherwise this is not possible. If a sick person exercises benevolence and spirituality with a view to be cured, his aim is defeated. This exercise must be carried out all the time, especially when a person is healthy, because, as I have pointed out, it is only when he is truly healthy that he can concentrate on benevolence and spirituality. To be healthy his food intake must be properly managed, not as a routine but as a necessity.

Inquiry

What is necessary and what is futile?

Statement

Whatever is good for the welfare of the individual, his family, his society, his country and humanity is a necessity and must be religiously and continuously carried out. Whatever is not required and is harmful to any body or bodies is futile and must be discontinued or stamped out.

Inquiry

Do you believe that we have failed to identify and carry out the necessities in our lives?

Statement

My belief that we, men, have failed has been prompted by certain criteria of modern-day living. Wherever I go, I notice good people praying. It is something to be proud of, but underneath our prayers there lies a hidden truth. What are we praying for? A child can answer this question. We are praying for peace, happiness, good health, wealth, freedom, security, prosperity, love, unity and justice, among others.

We are also praying for the cessation of hostilities around the world; for the cessation of famine, poverty, and diseases around the world; and for the cessation of natural disasters around the world. Why are we praying for all these and to whom are we praying? We ask our parents or providers for something we do not have. It is ridiculous to ask for something we already have. For example, if we have enough money it is either futile or unreasonable to ask for it. If we have enough food, we cannot ask for more. If we have sufficient clothes, obviously, we cannot ask for more. If we do, we are certainly being greedy because it means we want more than we can use. Greed must never be entertained, harboured or cherished because it is the cause of many of our miseries. For example, if we eat more than enough we become obese, which gives rise to a host of illnesses. When we become obese, we are constantly fighting our obesity.

We spend a lot of money to achieve our aim. We cannot have more money if we do not work more. No one is willing to work more. How can an obese person work more anyway? If we want more clothes too, we need more money. We must not forget that if we are constantly putting on or losing weight, we also constantly need new clothes. It is inevitable.

And again, for more clothes, we need more money. And again, for more money we need more work. No one wants to work more. A vicious circle! The same applies if we want more properties. Those who work more to achieve what they want, as opposed to what they need, are full of stress in this materialistic age.

Stress spoils our health. When this happened, our happiness is disturbed, our peace of mind is disturbed, our freedom is disturbed; because those who are unhealthy, stressed and unhappy are not free to enjoy life. Here again we must not forget that money is needed to restore our health. Another vicious circle!

It follows that if we want peace, happiness, freedom and the like – the very things we pray for – we must eliminate greed from our life. But greed is not the only base quality we must get rid of. We must get rid of all our base qualities, because they are the exterminators of our peace, happiness, good health, freedom and all that we pray for.

The truth about two of my beliefs is evident here. First, we need not pray to God for something we can redress, reform or restore ourselves. We pray to God only to give us the courage, inspiration and strength to do it. With His inspiration and blessing we are quite capable of getting rid of our base qualities and securing everything we have been praying for. Secondly, everything we have been praying for – that is, peace, happiness and freedom and so on – is obviously not in our possession, and to have these things we must turn to ourselves and not God. God only helps those who help themselves.

Ironically, we pray to God not to give us courage, inspiration, strength and His blessing, but to give us the peace, happiness and freedom that we ourselves are capable of establishing or bringing about.

Inquiry

Isn't there enough peace, happiness and freedom in our world?

Statement

Is there really? I assembled some people who were willing to give honest answers to this question. I asked a middle-class man earning a fair living: 'Are you at peace?'

He answered: 'No, I've a lot of stress at work. My boss is often angry. There is always traffic congestion when I'm going to work or when I'm returning from work. There is stress at home too. Children do not obey their parents half the time. I'm watching violence on TV every day.

'My neighbours are rowdy and noisy. My house has been burgled twice and my family lives in fear. My brothers and sisters are not getting on well. How can there be peace in my life?'

I asked a sick person who has everything but good health: 'Are you happy?'

He answered: 'No. I'm unable to eat what I like because of all sorts of restrictions necessitated by my illness. There are complications associated with my illness. I've pains all the time. I'm unable to do what I like. My children are threatening to admit me to a home because they say I'm a burden on them.

'Everyone wants to go on holiday but they cannot go unless a nurse is employed. My wife is under stress and she makes no bones about it. How can I be happy?'

I asked a magnate: 'Do you feel free?'

He answered: 'No, I've had to rely on my bodyguards from the time my wife was kidnapped and I had to pay a huge ransom to free her. I want to go places on my own, roam around on my own, drive around on my own, eat food from stalls sometimes, which I used to do before I became rich. I feel like a prisoner within my own compound. I've everything – good health, luxury, everything except freedom. There's no safety.

'I'm a target for the mafia. Fear is my constant companion. Two guards have already been shot. Freedom? Where can I find it?'

I asked an ex-prisoner, now a businessman: 'Do you think there is justice in our world?'

He answered, 'No. I was framed and jailed. I'm a victim of political injustice. I supported the opposition party. I'm being spied upon all the time. I have to offer bribes to get anything done.

'I know of many cases of corruption and injustice but I can't reveal them to anybody because now I'm not sure who my friends are and who my enemies are. Where is justice in the world in which we are living?'

I asked a poor man: 'Do you have any complaint in life or about life?'

He answered: 'Many. I can't afford to make ends meet. Everything is pricey. I can't send my children to a good school. I'm a victim of the society I live in because I'm poor. No respect is shown to me in places like hospitals and offices whenever I have to call on these places.

'I've a motorbike and I'm stopped by police every week. I live in the slums surrounded by hooligans. I work hard but I don't see the reward. How can I have no complaints in life?'

I asked a young person: 'Are you happy with the present world?'

He answered: 'At first I thought I was, but after listening to the others, I realised how ignorant I was about the world I am living in. I thought there was nothing wrong. I thought we had everything to enjoy ourselves. What else did we need? I realised that the happiness I was satisfied with was not real happiness.

'I'd like to live in a peaceful, free, happy, just and loving world; but how can we change our present world into the idyllic world you're talking about?'

These people were not talking for themselves or about themselves. They were representing millions who have the same views, the same feelings and the same complaints. It is obvious that we have no peace, happiness, good health, lasting wealth, safety or the will to get rid of our evil possessions, or genuine ways to acquire good qualities and good fortune.

If we had peace, we could not pray for more, yet we could pray that it lasted for ever. The same applies to things like happiness, good health and freedom. The exception is anything that is material and transient, like money. Everyone nowadays wants money and plenty of it. The more we have the more we want. The very rich also want more. They believe, like the poor, that money can buy anything. In fact, money can buy nothing that is everlasting and that brings real happiness. Unlike the other things we pray for, money can also bring all sorts of misery – indulgence in our lives leading to illness, corruption leading to immorality…

We, men and women, have created a world of materialism. Money matters. Nothing else matters as much. We want money for what? To eat, drink, make merry, buy expensive clothes every week, change cars as often as new models appear, make bombs and blow up people, or travel to the North Pole? Our true feelings are lost in this quest.

We pray for things like peace, happiness and freedom without knowing what they really are. Children fight with their parents for tangible and transient things, but never for peace, happiness and freedom. It is not their fault. We have brought them up like that. We give them whatever they want, not whatever they need.

We have created a world in which the real meaning of many words has changed just as the real reasons for what we have been asking or doing have changed. Houses were not built to protect us from thieves, burglars and assassins. They were built to protect us from the natural elements such as heat, rain and wind, and from animals and reptiles. Now we are not afraid of animals getting in our houses, we are afraid of human beings getting in. We built cupboards and wardrobes to prevent our belongings from being spoilt by insects and not to lock up our valuables. But nowadays we do not care much about insects, but we do care a lot about robbers.

Everything has changed. The peace, happiness and freedom the present young generation know are not the same as they were during our predecessors' days. They wanted freedom to taste the lasting joy of spirituality; we want freedom to enjoy the transient pleasures of materialism. There is a big difference between their freedom and ours.

Inquiry

Obviously, they were more spiritualistic than materialistic. What in your opinion made them more spiritualistic?

Statement

They were not hypocrites and pretenders like us. They genuinely believed in God or gods; in reward and punishment for good and bad deeds respectively, in sharing peace and prosperity with each other; in working for the welfare of all; in promoting and exercising good manners. And they believed in morality and integrity, in doing a fair day's work for a fair day's money, in securing a good future for their children; in respecting and protecting each other's values; and in the preservation of humanity. They did not pretend to know, they knew, that the duty of human beings was to uphold those beliefs by doing deeds accordingly.

Hence, they were genuinely pious, honest, civil, humble, diligent, peaceful, just and benevolent. These days we see many people acting piously in public but devilishly in private. Who wants to work hard these days or be humble? Who does not harbour any ill-will in his heart? Who is not prejudiced, arrogant or jealous? Who is God-fearing nowadays?

Who sincerely believes that God will punish him for his bad deeds? Who sincerely believes that God will reward him for his good deeds? Let everyone answer these questions for himself, but he must do it in all sincerity and not like a hypocrite.

Inquiry

Will you give me your answers sincerely and not like a hypocrite?

Statement

There is one pretence I cannot deny – that I am one of us. Let me first mention a few incidents that I have seen or personally experienced.

I have seen seven people taking half a day to dig a hole for a flag pole.

Almost daily I come across incidents highlighting anger from an adult or a child.

So often we hear terrorists saying their actions are condoned by God because they have followed God's words.

I once went to see a cabinet minister in his office. He was on the phone talking to someone with all due care and tact when he beckoned me in. When he put the receiver down, he swore at the person he had just talked to on the phone. 'The bastards think they've voted me in to do all their work.' And then he turned to me and very politely asked, 'What can I do for you, friend?'

We all believe God has granted us the gift to spread love, but we are all guilty of spreading hatred – if not always, at least sometimes during our life. That is why everyone has one or more enemies.

The incidents I have mentioned are not isolated ones. They are representative of a large section of the world's population. I cannot read what is in a person's mind, but he knows. I cannot judge him but he can judge himself. Let us all judge ourselves and see for ourselves whether we genuinely love and cherish all the people of all communities in the world, a proposition I have already made earlier.

Because most of our ancestors were uneducated, they were easily persuaded by the learned ones, or by the clever ones, to believe in the existence of God or gods. Believing in God also meant believing in reward for good deeds and punishment for bad deeds, which were carried out in heaven and hell. They believed in life after death, because if they did not, they could not believe in heaven and hell. Their belief inspired them to do good deeds and avoid bad ones. Good deeds have always been associated with spirituality and humanitarianism, with God and saints, whereas evil deeds have always been associated with the devil and sinners.

Our ancestors' belief in God was deep-rooted and unshake-able; our belief in God is half-hearted and shaky. Yet our belief in money-power is total. The two beliefs are completely different. True belief in God can only inspire us to do good deeds; belief in money-power is often the instigator of evil deeds. I must point out that overindulging in anything, harbouring greed, supporting and encouraging corruption and other things connected with money, are evil deeds. And as for spending money on making bombs to kill innocent people, that cannot be related to belief in God.

It is unfortunate that, being educated, we refuse to learn from our ancestors. We forget that we are strongly linked to them, as strongly as we are linked to the future generations, not only physically but also spiritually. Whether we accept it or not, they have passed on their instincts to us and we will also pass on ours to our progeny. However, we are ignoring many of these instincts and our progeny will ignore many of ours. Sadly, we are ignoring the good instincts such as their goodness, their benevolence and their piety, which are the true treasures of mankind. Ignoring them and believing in money-power has converted us from spirituality to materialism.

We fear nothing but our own kind. They were better than us, those people who feared God and the punishments for bad deeds. They did not fear their own kind. Here I must emphasise that I am writing about the people at the lower end of society. The people at the higher level were always in conflict probably because of their arrogance, hypocrisy, jealousy and their dominance. It is a pity that the influence of the people at the higher level and not that of those at the lower level has prevailed and spread globally.

People who believed in God and the Demon, and therefore, in heaven and hell, were more humanitarian than those who do not believe in heaven and hell nowadays. They did not have doubts about heaven and hell; we do. However, those who earnestly believe in heaven and hell these days *are* more humanitarian than those who do not. This is due to fear, the reverential fear of God.

Inquiry

Do you believe in heaven and hell?

Statement

When they stand for specific places where rewards and punishments are meted out after death, I do not believe in them. It is generally believed that those who do nothing evil go to heaven after death, and those who do all types of wicked deeds go to hell. If that is so, there must be very few inhabitants either in heaven or in hell. I do not believe that there have been many people who have done nothing evil to merit eternal bliss in heaven; or that there have been many people who have done such wicked deeds as to deserve to burn eternally in hell. If men were to mete out such rewards and punishments they would be considered too generous or too cruel.

If I believed in this 'heaven and hell' I would be constrained to associate God with these qualities, but I know God cannot be 'too generous' or 'too cruel'. I believe that God is simply and completely 'just'. Now, if there are only a few inhabitants of heaven and hell where have all the other dead people gone?

At this point I must admit I am a bit confused. I imagine all those possibilities that can offer me an answer. An intermediate realm between heaven and hell would have dispelled my confusion; or the theory that we really do not come from anywhere and do not go anywhere after death; or the belief that there are different degrees of reward and punishment in the same heaven or hell thus accommodating all the dead ones; or we are born only to eat, drink, sleep, enjoy life and die; or nothing really exists and the universe with all it contains is just an illusion.

If I analyse these five possibilities from an ordinary person's sense of reasoning and understanding, many more questions crop up. If there is a realm between heaven and hell is it not the earth we are inhabiting where we are all receiving varying degrees of reward and/or punishment? If so, we all died before we arrived here. If so, then where were we? If we were just born because nature necessitated it, why are we bothered about good or evil? Has God a hand in our creation?

Is there a God? If the world is an illusion, what is our role in it? Is it only to prove that it is an illusion? I do not believe that I am an illusion. I do not believe that the universe is an illusion.

I believe there is a God and He has created this universe. He has created us. He used the atoms and His energy to create the universe. He used our souls and the atoms and His energy to create us. He has created us to embellish His universe. We are His employees.

He had to make rules for us. He had to make these rules equitable, unchanging and perfect for ever. We are all bound by His rules, just like we are bound by the rules of our countries. There is only one difference: God's rules never change; men's rules do. His rules relating to our birth and death are contained in His Law of Karma. The simple and efficient way it functions is stunning. It is so easy for anybody to understand. As we sow, so we reap. Good actions reward us; wicked actions punish us. Some are born princes; some are born paupers. Some enjoy good health, good homes, good fortune; others are inflicted with poverty, pain and persecution from the moment of their birth. When did we sow the seeds of our rewards or our punishments?

Or is it God who has unfairly subjected some to punishment and others to enjoyment? And if we have not paid for our sins in this life, when do we pay for them? If we have not been rewarded for our good deeds in this life, when will we be rewarded? It follows that we have sown the seeds of rewards or punishments before we were born, and we will collect the reward or punishment for the seeds we are sowing now. Where were we before we were born? It could not have been in heaven or in hell because we believe that once we enter these places we never come out of them.

Where are we going after death? It cannot be heaven or hell, because if it is, then what happens to us after we have been rewarded or have paid for our sins?

The only possible and plausible solution to cure my confusion is, I believe, the Law of Karma. Everything is here, on this earth, as long as the cycle or our births and deaths is not dissolved. Heaven is a state and not a place, and so is hell. Great happiness is heaven; great pain is hell. When we have surmounted both, we achieve salvation.

If a layperson tries to understand God and His laws beyond this, he will have to aspire to be a scholar in his next birth. I am trying. I am also trying urgently to warn the world that it is not too late for us to reform our society, our education, our morality, our piety and our attitudes and mentality. The world has become too chaotic, but there are ways to undo the chaos.

These are the most obvious culprits of our chaotic world:

1. Stress resulting from our dislike of work and our ambition to make money quickly.

2. Fear of thugs and criminals, diseases, fanatics, terrorists and suicide bombers, corrupt and cruel dictators, rioters, discrimination and persecution.

3. Mobile phones which do not allows us to:

    a. sleep in peace;

    b. have meals in peace in restaurants or at home;

    c. holiday in peace;

    d. travel in peace;

    e. relax in peace;

> f. attend lectures, conferences and other gatherings in peace;
>
> g. enjoy nature in peace;
>
> h. watch a movie in peace.

They have become man's best friends.

4. Computer games on which our children are hooked and because of which their human feelings are severely impaired.

5. Materialism, which has taken over our lives completely.

6. Rotten politicians creating rotten governments.

7. Impatience giving rise to anger and violence.

8. Arrogance and domineering attitudes.

9. Selfishness and denial of humbleness.

10. Mindlessness.

11. Decline of humanitarianism and breakdown of human relationships globally.

12. Hypocrisy.

Once we get rid of these culprits the chaos will eliminate itself. Of course, some of the above are culprits because we have made them so. For example, mobile phones are very useful but we often misuse them or overuse them. We believe they keep us in contact with our nearest and dearest. This is true but I feel we must visit our nearest and dearest more often. There is no real substitute for spending some time together with our friends, relatives or neighbours.

The warmth and cordiality of keeping company can never be equalled by telephone conversations, no matter how many times we phone. This is clearly observed in the case of two lovers, or a mother and her children, or two friends. They need to meet, because they are not happy with just phone conversations. You cannot share a meal over the phone. You cannot have the real feeling of a caress over the phone.

Children's computer games can be made useful by substituting violence and fiction with rectitude and reality.

Materialism must exist and must not be allowed to supersede or exceed spirituality. The triumph of materialism over spirituality has distanced us from lasting happiness, freedom and peace. We must bring materialism under our control and under the control of our spirituality, then we will succeed in our aim.

Let us suppose we have achieved true happiness, freedom, and peace in a united world. We must not become too complacent and do nothing to preserve our achievement. We must ensure that we, and the future generations, will enjoy it for ever, and not brood over and resent the sacrifices we have made to secure it. We must be firm in our minds about it right now. We must plan what we want to achieve: that is, true happiness, freedom and peace in the world; what we will do with our achievement, how we will preserve it; how we will improve it, and how we will teach and motivate our progeny to keep its flame alive all the time.

We must know what we are making sacrifices for and whether we shall be able to appreciate it when we have secured it. If we are not sure, or if we are sure we will not appreciate it, then we must not engage in a struggle to attain it. It is also very important that we make ourselves worthy to enjoy true happiness, freedom and peace. This must be our first priority.

Up to now, we have been acting like children who fight or beg their parents for toys and games, which they spoil in no time after they get them. They are forgiven for their actions, for they are children, after all. But how can adults be forgiven if they behave like children? And that is exactly what we have been doing for a long time. After conquering a country, the colonisers did not know how to cherish it and keep it for long. After fighting so resolutely for independence, people start fighting among themselves instead of establishing peace and freedom in their countries. After being freed from slavery, we have knowingly become slaves of drugs, diseases, drink, vice, money and materialism. At the individual level, we are worse. A person achieves a university degree and everyone hopes he will work for the welfare of all, but his degree is only for his own benefit. He is only interested in earning money with it. A couple get married after lengthy, strenuous and elaborate preparation for their wedding, but they do not know how to continuously improve their relationship after marriage. They do not know how to raise their children. The many ill-mannered, neglected or overprotected children, and the many divorces or broken marriages seen around, are living proof.

We listen to lectures, discourses and sermons on morality but what do we do after that? Do we improve our life with them? We have many achievements in our lives but we do not value, use or preserve them permanently or properly. Nothing is achieved overnight or with ease. Time, sacrifice, willpower, perseverance, sincerity and the right reason for achieving a goal are all very important. But it is more important to properly care for our desired achievement. To achieve global happiness, freedom, prosperity, justice, and peace we must all sacrifice a lot and work together towards our goal. Once we have achieved it, we must not treat it as a temporary arrangement. It won't be a five-year plan. It will be a permanent arrangement. It is imperative that we understand and agree to this before we embark on a collective effort to achieve an ideal *modus vivendi*.

Summary

How can we create an idyllic world of peace, prosperity, happiness, justice and piety for everyone? The answer lies in the following:

1. Education. Education is most important. Besides the ongoing education, there is a need for global compulsory education on good conduct and manners and it must include oral, written and practical examinations at all stages of life. If we start straightaway, the result will be visible in the third generation from now. The idyllic condition will prevail from the fifth generation from now. This will lead to...

2. A change in the attitude and mentality of people. Once the individual is educated from before or from birth, his mentality, attitude and behaviour will become automatically noble. Nobleness will lead to...

3. Obligatory and voluntary duties by the individual who will not be stressed, angry or lazy. He will be mentally and physically healthy thus saving the state health department a colossal amount of money. The individual will not be greedy in any aspect of life. Food-wise, he will eat only what his body requires. Thus there will be enough food for the rest of the world to share. He will not amass wealth, thus leaving enough for the world to share. He will indulge in all actions that promote the welfare of all. He will practise, preserve and promote...

4. Humanitarianism which is the seat of ideal human relationships, love, service to mankind, peace, prosperity, understanding, justice and equality, and the weapon to eliminate corruption, violence, crime, decadence, irreligion, terrorism and war. It will give birth to...

5. Happiness and piety in the inhabitants of the world, and to...

6. Environmental protection. There will be a sustained effort by each individual to maintain a healthy environment. There will be no need to designate an environmental day as each day will be one. There will be...

7. Law and order. Each individual will help keep and protect law and order as there will be discipline globally. This will assist...

8. Good governance throughout the world, and there will be...

9. A harmonious fusion of secular and religious practices.

10. Spirituality and global harmony will reign supreme.

Lightning Thoughts

A smile never dies.

∽

You can rebel against reason but you cannot defeat it.

∽

In courtship, a couple always have too much to say; in matrimony it is often too little.

∽

If you want your love to thrive or survive, do not run after wealth.

∽

A prospective employer asked a group of jobseekers: 'Who wants a job?'

Everyone raised their hands.

Then he asked them, 'Who wants to work?'

No one raised their hands.

∽

Far more people want to be heard than want to hear. Consequently, there are more preachers than disciples, more teachers than students and more politicians than electors.

∽

Students with bad manners rarely succeed in their studies; that is why they must be taught ethics first and then all the other subjects.

∽

A wildebeest that abandons its herd is likely to be prey to several predators. A human being who abandons his society is similarly prey to many predators such as loneliness, exploitation, rejection and ignorance.

All is not well in the home of someone who is seeking peace of mind outside.

A dispute between two individuals, or between an individual and a community, or between two communities, can always be resolved by the law of humanity, relationships and reason, but never by the law of paradox, obstinacy and ignorance.

When conscience and logic are in conflict, there is mental confusion, but it is logic that ultimately triumphs.

The day before yesterday, I saw many fathers planting fruit trees for their children.

Yesterday I saw many fathers walking with their children to the fruit trees.

Today I see many fathers literally carrying their children and resting them on the fruit trees.

Tomorrow I shall see many fathers stampeding with their children on their shoulders to the fruit trees.

The day after tomorrow there will be too many fathers and too many children, but there will be fewer fruit trees because no one has planted a fruit tree since the day before yesterday. The fathers and the children will fight for the fruit trees.

Psst! I just heard that once upon a time, the mind was quicker than the tongue. Now the phenomenon is rare.

Truth has never been a topic for gossipers.

Nowadays, in all stages at school, provided there are enough worthy teachers, children must be taught ethics and etiquette, good conduct and courtesy, and the values and virtues of life so they can teach their preceding and their future generations the knowledge they have acquired.

The past we cannot change, the present we have to live with, the future we can mould.

To understand a terrorist, one must stoop to his level: one must become ignorant.

Corrupt politicians are thieves who empty the pockets of the people to fill their own. Good politicians are gods who empty their own pockets to fill those of the poor people.

How to recognise a corrupt politician: he becomes rich overnight.

There is no guarantee that he who defects today will not defect again tomorrow.

A genuine spouse honours their vows.

In the mathematics of family, the sum total is constantly one, no matter how many ones are added to one.

No one wants to be harmed. If you do not harm someone, you will not be harmed by someone.

If, as human beings, it is difficult to solve our problems and settle our differences, as animals, it will be impossible.

If you want a job done, do not wait for others to make the first move.

If you feel hurt because you have been falsely and wrongly accused, then you have not got rid of your pride.

(A disguised event.) While taking a long walk in the city, I lost my way. I met a gentleman and asked him for directions to my hotel. He sensed I was thirsty as well. He politely asked me to come to his house to quench my thirst and then he would show me the way. I followed him while chatting.

His house was as pleasing as his hospitable nature. He asked me to sit in his magnificent lounge while he fetched me a juice. While he was getting it, his son entered the lounge. He was around twelve years old.

'What are you doing here?' he asked me abruptly.

'What are you doing here?' I replied pleasantly, thinking that he was as gentle as his father.

'This is my house. Go away!' he shouted rudely, much to my surprise.

'Don't talk to your guest like that, son,' the gentleman requested from the kitchen.

'Go away, you ugly man,' the son shouted, hurling his toy gun at me. 'This is not your house.'

The gentleman returned to the lounge and gave me a glass of juice. I took a few sips and placed the glass on the coffee table. His son purposefully knocked it over. The father asked the son to leave the lounge.

'No,' he shouted. 'Tell that man to go away.'

On the way out, the gentleman showed me the way to my place and very humbly apologised for his son's behaviour.

'He deserves a sharp slap, that boy,' he told me. 'He's so rude.'

I smiled and left, wishing the boy was as polite as his father, but knowing that the boy was not to blame and it was his father who deserved a sharp slap for not disciplining his son from the moment of his birth.

A poor country with peaceful people is better than a rich country with feuding people, but a rich country with peaceful people is best.

When I was a small boy, my mother told me a story because she wanted me to think before I spoke. When God made man, He asked him if he wanted to bathe or eat more often.

'To eat and drink,' man replied.

So, God granted him his wish.

Thus, man trapped himself because he has to work for his food all the time.

A person does not visit someone at home when they know they are not in, unless that person is a thief.

You do not achieve excellence because you have won a gold medal. You earn a gold medal because you have achieved excellence.

Sometimes what we do with good intentions turns out to be a disservice.

A little boy once caught a young robin that was taking shelter in his room from a cyclone. He kept it in a comfortable cage and tended it with love. When the cyclone had passed the boy did not release it lest it was again caught in bad weather, and also because he found it so beautiful that he wanted to keep it as a pet. The sad robin died after a few days.

'I had all the love and comfort,' it peeped before dying, 'but I had no freedom.'

Doing something good prevents us from doing anything bad.

Despite his good intention to create a superhuman being, Frankenstein created a monster. Like him, also with good intentions, we have created the present world (a lot bigger than his monster), which is eating human beings by the thousand every day through war, famine, disease, murder, environmental pollution and destruction and mass hatred, all of which are correlated and interlinked.

ও

I went to visit my stressed friend, Dino, at his factory where he had employed some twenty workers. He took me on a conducted tour of his factory. He noticed a couple of spanners lying on the floor where they should not have been.

'Bora!' he shouted.

Bora left his post and came over.

'Yes, Mr Dino?' he replied.

'Didn't I tell you to put those spanners away?' Dino raved. 'Why haven't you done it?'

'Sorry, sir. I'll do it straightaway.'

'You'd better, you idiot.'

'I'm fed up with repeating to these bastards what they should do,' Dino told me, looking furious.

We continued our tour, at the end of which Dino asked me what I thought of his prosperous business.

'You've done well,' I replied. 'You'll do better in the future, provided...' I hesitated.

'Provided what?' he asked me curiously.

'Provided you control your anger,' I told him.

'It's not possible as long as these idiots are working for me,' Dino said. 'They're stupid. They're destructive. They're useless. And they're argumentative even when they know they're wrong.'

'That's why you're the employer and they're the employees,' I told him. 'Once you understand this, you'll all be happier and your business will flourish more. A happy atmosphere increases productivity. After all, they do your work despite their limitations and despite your anger and outbursts. Besides, anger causes more stress and vice versa. Both promote illnesses. It is, therefore, in the interests of all to control your anger.'

'Thank you, my friend,' Dino said. 'I'll take your advice.'
Dino is now a big businessman.

Just as an inferiority complex is ingrained in women's psyche, a superiority complex is ingrained in men's. It will take a long time for these complexes to equal out.

Light is truth, light is love, light is hope and light is life.

Those who do not know the meaning of marriage, but want to marry, must not spend great sums on extravagant marriage preparations, rites and rituals, as their marriages are not likely to last. Logically, they must not marry.

When you are good and everyone is like you, you will never be a social outcast. When you are good and everyone else is bad, you are made an outcast just like someone who is bad when everyone else is good. But there is a significant difference. When good people cast out a bad one from their circle, it is normally after all their attempts to improve him have failed. When bad people cast out a good one from their circle, it is normally because he attempts to improve them.

Many people believe because they are uneducated they have been victims of the 'Divide and Rule' policy devised by the imperial rulers. Now educated people are fostering and abetting the same policy, but with an appendage: 'Divide, Weaken, Rule and Destroy'. This is instead of getting on with the task of building and consolidating their countries and their nations.

Any religion founded on an idea drawn from the Religion of Truth is fragile. Only the Religion of Truth is unshakeable, just like God, who is the source of all existence.

Good conduct, manners and behaviour are the vitamins of education; discipline, willpower and creativity are its minerals. Survival is impossible without them. Just as the body cannot be healthy without vitamins and minerals, education cannot be complete without the above virtuous qualities. It is, therefore, imperative that we include these qualities in our education.

Our good manners delight our neighbours; our bad manners irritate or offend them. Since we must live in harmony with our neighbours, it behoves us to cultivate good manners. Irritating or offending our neighbours creates bad relationships, animosity and instability in the neighbourhood. When this happens, no one can live in peace.

Good manners are a quality that is appreciated by one and all. It generates friendship and love and attracts respect and praise. Good manners, however basic, are great; for example, greeting everyone with a smile.

If a person's behaviour is repulsive in any way, that means bad manners. It does not command respect and breeds hatred; for example, swearing at others.

If we beautify our country with the marvels of modern technology and the wonders of modern landscaping in parks and gardens, and not our people with the natural qualities of mankind, we will be casting pearls before swine and defeating our progress. It is like greeting someone with a smile on your face while your heart is full of hatred, like a true hypocrite.

No one is born a criminal. A criminal is grown by men.

We shall find it difficult to change our mentality and attitude because they have stayed with us for too long and we are too attached to them, but if we raise our children with the right attitude and mentality, they will find them natural and easy to live with. We must accept our blunders and stop our delusions instead of inculcating them into our children, who are not to be blamed if they are misled.

The religio-cultural societies can survive as long as the government of the state and the religion of the individual do not contradict one another. Both must be founded upon truth, logic and humanitarianism. We must not confuse our children with the illogical and ridiculous stories of our scriptures. They were written by very clever people to convince the uneducated people at the time of writing. These stories must now be considered obsolete. We are educated people and we will be insulting our intelligence and reasoning if we believe in them.

Ironically, many well-educated and learned scholars believe in them, preach them and confuse our children, hence their apathy towards true religion and their obsession with materialism.

Men have developed a knack for harbouring and practising unfounded doctrines that breed the wrong attitude, and undesirable idiosyncrasies such as fanaticism, superstition, segregation, prejudice, superiority or inferiority complexes, arrogance, dominance, injustice and racism, among others. Such doctrines must be tabooed.

Impatience provokes anger sometimes; oppression most of the time; and offence all the time. Therefore, it behoves everyone to cultivate patience and not haste; humbleness and not arrogance; tolerance and not inconsideration.

Individual anger can provoke violence and illness; collective anger often provokes violence and barbarity.

One cannot be humble if one is not merciful and vice versa.

❧

If you commit an act that offends others, you must refrain from doing it again lest the same act is done by others to offend you. If you are defending a just cause, you must not refrain from doing so whether it is for yourself or for others, otherwise you are partial and fanatical. Only fools and fanatics are offended by an act that they think will not offend others if they do it to them.

❧

If you offend others you have no right to believe you are a peaceful person.

❧

There are only two types of catastrophe in our world: natural, such as tsunamis, earthquakes, volcanoes, floods and hurricanes, and man-made, such as war, disease, famine, terrorism, and religion, among others. Hypocritically, we are more concerned about natural catastrophes, which have fewer victims than man-made ones. We refuse to accept that there is little if anything we can do to avert natural catastrophes, whereas we can do a lot to avert man-made catastrophes. We also refuse to believe that we do not know where and when natural catastrophes will strike, and that we know where and when man-made catastrophes will strike. How two-faced we are!

❧

I was strolling along a village road when I came across a bar. It was quite boisterous inside, so I was curious to find out how the villagers enjoyed themselves. I went in. There were some thirty customers inside, all eating, drinking, smoking and making merry while having big arguments about politics.

'Great!' I said to myself. 'They're all happy and keeping themselves occupied.'

I realised they were all men, most of them married. Their wives were waiting at home to eat with them.

'My friends,' I addressed them, 'I'm glad that you're all having a great time. So you must. There are two questions I want to ask. First, what about your wives? Secondly, why can't you take some time for social, cultural and devotional duties?'

130

One guy, probably the most audacious and respected one, replied, 'Listen, my friend. We work all day long. We work hard. We need some sort of relaxation and we find it here. This is our life: work, a few moments here, go home and sleep after dinner with our wives. What's wrong in that?'

'Nothing really,' I replied. 'You're being selfish though. You're not being constructive. I suggest you find some time to go along with your family to some devotional, religious and cultural gatherings.'

'No, we can't ever,' replied one of them. 'This is the only time we can spare, and if we don't use it here, we'll go crazy after a hard day's work.'

'You won't if you attend a good devotional session instead of this,' I replied.

'I don't think so,' one of them retorted. 'This is the best way to unwind.'

I did not argue, because we were talking on different levels, which they could not fathom.

I left the bar and continued my stroll. I came across another bar from which the same din emerged. I went in there, and to the surprise of all twenty customers, I proposed: 'In two months, I am organising a trip to Europe for six weeks. I want thirty volunteers. I'll pay all expenses for fares, accommodation, food, transfers and tours. How many of you want to join me? Please raise your hands.'

All except one raised their hands. I asked the one who did not, 'Don't you want to come along?'

'I do,' he replied, 'but I can't come without my wife and my parents.'

'Suppose I pay for them too?' I asked.

'Then we'll all come.'

Straightaway the others wanted their wives, parents and relatives to be included in the trip.

'OK!' I said. 'I'll pay for all of them.'

'Then we'll all come,' the leader said.

Funny, isn't it? They had no time to attend devotional meetings, but not only did they find time to be on a trip for six weeks but they also arranged, without consultation, to find time for their relatives.

Once upon a time, there was a father who generously gave sound advice to his children. They did not listen to him. One day he had a fall and lost his voice. They yearned for it to return.

In our reverie, reflection and reality,
We must not harbour hatred and hostility.
Love we must, piety, justice and humanity,
And establish happiness, peace and liberty.

If man could control his palate, he would be healthier, richer and happier; if he could control his ambition, he would be more peaceful, freer and dutiful.

Anger is the most fatal disease manufactured by and attacking the very person who displays it.

❧

Humble people are healthier than conceited and arrogant ones because they are rarely angry and almost always calm. Arrogance fosters anger and aggression and gives rise to hypertension and heart disease.